The McGraw-Hill
Desk Reference
for
Editors, Writers,
and Proofreaders

The McGraw-Hill Desk Reference
for
Editors, Writers,
and Proofreaders

K.D. Sullivan and
Merilee Eggleston

New York Chicago San Francisco Lisbon London Madrid Mexico City
Milan New Delhi San Juan Seoul Singapore Sydney Toronto

4 5 6 7 8 9 10 11 12 13 14 15 16 17 18 19 20 21 22 23 24   FGR/FGR   0 9 8

ISBN-13: 978-0-07-147000-1 (book and CD package)
ISBN-10:   0-07-147000-X (book and CD package)

ISBN-13: 978-0-07-147001-8 (book alone)
ISBN-10:   0-07-147001-8 (book alone)

Library of Congress Control Number: 2006921061

Interior design by Nick Panos

McGraw-Hill books are available at special quantity discounts to use as premiums and sales promotions, or for use in corporate training programs. For more information, please write to the Director of Special Sales, Professional Publishing, McGraw-Hill, Two Penn Plaza, New York, NY 10121-2298. Or contact your local bookstore.

This book is printed on acid-free paper.

*For Mom, John, Tawni, Taevin, and Boomer—who
all make my heart smile
—K.D.*

*For my parents, for Jere, and for everyone who
makes words matter
—Merilee*

Contents

PART TWO The 3 Cs: What to Look for as You Work

Preface

Editors are everywhere. The people who spot errors and keep language clear are not just in publishing houses, poring over the next bestseller. They're in offices on Main Street and cubicles in Silicon Valley; they're at front desks everywhere and home offices anywhere. They're polishing a report, reviewing a memo, proofreading a Web site. They're perfecting their own work or troubleshooting someone else's. Editors are everyone who works to be sure that writing is correct, consistent, and clear—and, at its best, *compelling*.

If you're one of those people, you're an editor, and this book is for you. We hope you'll consider it a trusted mentor and keep it close at hand. Whether you have editorial experience or not, you'll learn how to spot problems in any written work, and what to do once you've found them. You'll learn the process of editing—how to identify project parameters, how to mark changes and ask authors questions, and, of course, what to look for as you edit.

You'll also learn some things the easy way that we've learned the hard way over our combined several decades of squinting at words. We've included as many tips from the real editorial world as we could squeeze in, an entire section to help you master electronic editing, and even some pointers for editing specialized material.

You'll find some interesting extras in Appendix B, including an editing test you might want to take, just for fun, before reading the book (but no peeking at the answer key!) and then again after you finish, to marvel at your new expertise. You'll also find, throughout the book, a collection of practical tools to transfer to your own desktop and use, *now*.

No matter where you work or what kind of writing you need to improve, this book will help you achieve every editor's goal: to make sure nothing stands between the writer's message and the reader's mind.

Acknowledgments

I want to thank my coauthor, Merilee, for her years of making me look good. We've worked together for more than a decade, and she's always able to take my ideas and make them shine even more than I could—adding her own knowledge and creativity, thinking of things I never would have. This book was inspired by a group of editorial job aids I wanted to create for my company and my clients, and Merilee kindly and expertly helped me to develop them and now incorporate them into this book.

I'm also grateful to every colleague and every client who asked for advice on how to write or edit electronically and for every problem-solving opportunity they presented, which prompted me to want to find easier ways to do what we do and do it well.

And in particular, I want to thank Karen Mead for her hours of brainstorming and friendly ear during the process of creating this book, along with her practical and expert advice on the electronic and specialty editing chapters. Thank you also to Frances Stack, Scott Apostolou, and Jan Seger for their contributions to the chapters on editing PDFs, PowerPoint files, and Web content; and to our excellent agent Grace Freedson for her introduction to Karen Young and McGraw-Hill, and for ten years of being in my corner. I also had the joy—for the second time—of working with our editor Craig Bolt. He had such a great sense of what we wanted to say and maintained our voice and our goal through the editing and production of this book. And special thanks to Karen Young, for her vision and diligence in championing this book—what a champion she was, and is.

—K.D. SULLIVAN

This book started with a modest vision—some job aids for people who work with words—and grew to include much more. In many ways, it reflects the most vital things we've learned during each of our careers. So I'd like to start with a nod to some of the people who have shaped my career and made it possible.

I would first like to thank my parents, who believed in education, who taught by example, and who from the time I could talk answered my every question thoughtfully and in complete sentences.

I would also like to thank Jerry Keenan, the generous editor and mentor who trusted me with my first book project; the authors who have graciously allowed me to mark up their prose and have taught me to be a better editor in the process; my coauthor, K.D., who has opened doors I never would have found, promoted my work, and given me so many opportunities to learn; and always my husband, Jere, for his endless love, patience, and support no matter how late the hour or how tight the deadline.

Finally, I'd like to heartily second K.D.'s gratitude to all the bright, dedicated people who gave their time, energy, and expertise to this book, both while we were writing it and during its editing and production. Every one of them proved what we firmly believe—that there's nothing like another set of eyes and a fresh perspective to improve the finished product.

—MERILEE EGGLESTON

PART ONE

Gearing Up to Edit

Before you actually sit down to edit a piece of writing, you need to gear up.

You need to know some details about the project, about what's expected of

you, and some basics about how to do your job. The two chapters in this part

will prepare you to do your best work with no wasted motion.

Before You Begin

Stop. Set down your red pencil. Move away from the keyboard. Before you read the first word or mark the first change, there are things about every editorial project you should know.

What Level of Work Will You Do?

Is it your job simply to snag typos and catch foot-tall faux pas in grammar, or will you need to check facts, reword, reorder, and generally revamp the writing to make it the best it can be? There's a big difference—and many levels of editorial effort—between the two approaches, and you shouldn't begin until you know what's wanted.

Editorial tasks fall on a continuum, with proofreading at one end and substantive editing at the other. Generally, in proofreading, the goal is editorial accuracy; in editing, it's accuracy *and* improvement. Here's how the levels of editorial review differ:

- **Standard proofreading** involves making sure writing is free of mechanical errors—in spelling, punctuation, consistency, and some elements of formatting—and is grammatically correct.
- **Editorial proofreading** encompasses all the tasks in standard proofreading, plus a few minor tweaks to ensure clarity and correct word choice.
- **Copyediting** involves all proofreading tasks and also improves phrasing and organization to make the writing more effective.
- **Substantive editing** calls for a greater level of rewriting and reorganization and even for suggesting new approaches and ideas.

Here's a single sentence, edited at the four different levels:

Original text: *What makes a good editing jobs into a grate editing job, is keeping both the rules and the reader in mind.*

Standard proofreading: *What makes a good editing job into a great editing job is keeping both the rules and the reader in mind.*

Editorial proofreading: *What turns a good editing job into a great editing job is keeping both the rules and the reader in mind.*

Copyediting: *Keeping the reader as well as the rules in mind is what turns a good editing job into a great one.*

Substantive editing: *Good editors apply the rules of writing; great ones do it with the reader in mind.*

Ideally, large editorial changes are made early on, followed by proofreading later to catch small items that editors may have overlooked or that were introduced along the way.

But the world of writing is rarely ideal. Very often, time is short, money is tight, and editorial work must be prioritized. Also, not every piece of writing needs a serious overhaul. The level of your edit will depend on several things— what the writing needs, what the budget will allow, how the writing will be used, and most important, *what you've been asked to do.*

If you're perfecting your own writing, at your own expense, and time is unlimited, you can edit at whatever level seems right. You have no one to consider but yourself and your readers.

Or if you've been asked to do major repairs to someone else's writing, by someone who knows how long it will take and what it will cost, you can strive for picture-perfect prose.

But in most cases, practical factors will determine the level of editorial review. Every editing project is differ-

Note: This book is for everyone who cleans up, clears up, smooths out, or reworks words, at any level, but that's a mouthful, so when we say "edit," "editor," or "editing," we almost always mean "proofread," "proofreader," and "proofreading," too.

ent, and each has its own needs and constraints. A memo that's purely informational, with a limited audience and brief life span, probably doesn't merit the kind of editorial scrutiny you'd give a quarterly report to shareholders or a biography of a world leader. Sometimes a piece is so clean and well written that there's no need to do more than the lightest proofread. Other times a piece is so technical that there's little room to edit without changing meanings. Whoever assigns you the editing task will usually let you know how much—or how little—work you're to do. If that person doesn't, be sure to ask.

For more on editing levels and what's called for at each, see Chapter 5.

Who Is the Audience?

It's vitally important for an editor to know the intended audience for a piece of writing. Why? If you know who will read it, you'll know whether to ask the author to explain the concept of cost basis or just let her sail right on to annualized yield. If the reader is a financial professional, it would seem a bit patronizing to include a primer on those basics. But if the reader is your next-door neighbor (and he doesn't have a seat on the stock exchange), you'll need to be sure the author explains—simply and clearly—what such terms mean.

When you know who the reader will be, you can gauge whether the vocabulary, style, and depth of the material are appropriate or if different words, explanations, or presentation are needed.

When Is It Due?

An editing project's due date affects several things—how you pace yourself, the scope of work possible in the available time, and often the cost of the project.

The best way to determine how long a project will take is to edit several representative pages to see how quickly you finish them. Knowing that, you can fairly accurately calculate how much time you'll need to complete the whole project.

Tip

If you can't edit sample pages, use this rule of thumb to estimate time: for a medium level of editing, assuming two complete readings, figure four to six 8½-by-11-inch or 250-word pages per hour. For a lighter edit, the pace will be faster; for a heavier edit, it will be slower. To be most effective, try not to edit for more than six hours a day.

If you've been given a deadline, and according to your calculations it will be difficult to deliver the work on time, you have three options:

- Work more hours per day or more days per week
- Reduce the scope of the work (say, from copyediting to an editorial proofread)
- Try to get the deadline altered

Discuss these alternatives with whoever has asked you to do the work and do it just as soon as you think you might face a time crunch. If the choice is to burn midnight or weekend oil to make the deadline, the overtime hours could add to the cost of the project. Be sure that's understood. If the choice is to reduce the scope of the work, be sure you and whoever makes that choice are in clear agreement on what items will not be reviewed or improved as a result.

What Format Is It In?

Is your editing project in hard copy or in electronic format? The answer can affect the way you'll receive and deliver the work, how you'll mark changes, and how you'll attach questions as you go.

Work that's in hard copy almost always started out as an electronic file (such as a Microsoft Word or an Adobe PDF file), so if you'd prefer to work electronically, be sure to ask for that file. Sometimes you really will need to work on hard copy (say, on a printout of a Web page), but most writing today is done using word processing software, and most editing is done the same way.

Tip

While most people who write use computer software, not all of them are familiar with the editorial markup tools their program includes. Before you start editing, be sure the person who will review your work is comfortable with the way you'll be marking changes and inserting questions. (For much more on electronic editing, see Part Three.)

Which References Will You Use?

Most editors rely on the most recent version of *The Chicago Manual of Style* to steer them through style choices (*president* or *President*?), punctuation pitfalls (period inside or outside quotes?), and grammar's gray areas (*like* or *as*?). Most also let the latest *Merriam-Webster's Collegiate Dictionary* have the final say on spelling, capitalization, and hyphenation.

Some organizations prefer other resources, however, either instead of these standbys or in addition to them. Magazines and newspapers generally adhere to *The Associated Press Stylebook*, for instance, and some pundits prefer *The American Heritage Dictionary of the English Language*. Before you begin an editing project, be sure to verify which reference books you're expected to use.

Be sure, also, to ask if a *style sheet* already exists for the project or for the department or organization that created the writing. A style sheet is simply a listing of things an editor needs to remember and keep consistent while working on a piece of writing—spellings, capitalizations, abbreviations, punctuation, number and formatting conventions, and anything else that crops up repeatedly. It is an editor's faithful ally and the best way to ensure consistency in your work. By all means, inquire about any existing style sheets and use them. (For more on reference sources and style sheets, see Chapter 2.)

Who Will Answer Your Questions?

Inevitably, you'll have questions as you edit. Style manuals, style sheets, dictionaries, and the Web will answer some of them, but you'll need a real live person to answer others.

Before you start your work, find out whom to contact with queries and how. Be sure you have all appropriate phone numbers, fax numbers, and e-mail addresses for your project's decision maker(s), including contact information for nights and weekends if you'll be working during those times. (For more on effective querying, see Chapter 2.)

> **Tip**
> Nothing stands to save you more time (or frustration or expense) than a firm, early grasp of project parameters. The few minutes it takes to ask the right questions (the ones in this chapter!) can save hours or days of avoidable do-overs.

Tools

Project Information Checklist

Fill in this checklist before each project you edit or proofread to be sure you have all the start-up information you need:

Project Information Checklist

Project title: _____

Level of work requested:
- ☐ Standard proofread
- ☐ Editorial proofread
- ☐ Copyedit
- ☐ Substantive edit
- ☐ Other _____

Audience:
- ☐ Professional/specialized
- ☐ General
- ☐ Other _____

Due date/time: _____

Format of material:
- ☐ Hard copy
- ☐ Microsoft Word
- ☐ Adobe PDF
- ☐ Other _____

Preferred markup method: _____

_____

Preferred reference sources: _____

_____

Existing style sheet(s)?
- ☐ Yes
- ☐ No

Contact information: _____

_____

2

Techniques and Tools

Yes, we *know* you're eager to dive into your document now that your mission is clear. But wait just a bit longer. First, spend some time setting up shop.

Like any trade, editorial work has basic techniques and tools that make the finished product easier to create and higher in quality. They don't take long to master, and they can make the difference between a smooth path to a great result and a bumpy ride to a mixed one. Here's how to edit like a pro:

Consult the Experts

No editor or proofreader lifts a pencil or touches a mouse without a few essential reference works at the ready. At minimum, you should have:

- *Merriam-Webster's Collegiate Dictionary*, eleventh edition (to check spellings, capitalizations, and hyphenations)
- *The Chicago Manual of Style*, 15th edition (for guidance on grammar, usage, punctuation, names, titles, numbers, and a thousand other details)

After these two, the universe of optional extras expands. Here are some of the brightest stars in it:

- *The American Heritage Dictionary of the English Language*
- *The Associated Press Stylebook*
- *The Careful Writer*, by Theodore M. Bernstein
- *The Copyeditor's Handbook*, by Amy Einsohn
- *Edit Yourself*, by Bruce Ross-Larson
- *The Elephants of Style*, by Bill Walsh

- *Garner's Modern American Usage*, by Bryan A. Garner
- *The Gremlins of Grammar*, by Toni Boyle and K.D. Sullivan
- *Woe Is I*, by Patricia T. O'Conner
- *Word Court*, by Barbara Wallraff
- *Words Into Type*, 3rd edition, by Marjorie E. Skillin and Robert M. Gay

In the last chapter we alerted you to a couple of these (*The Associated Press Stylebook* and *The American Heritage Dictionary of the English Language*), and you'll find more worthy reference sources in "For Reference and Reading" at the back of the book. As we've already said, some clients may ask you to make something other than *Chicago* or *Webster's* your primary resource. But even if they don't, you'll want another opinion from time to time.

Why? Two reasons. First, because while all these sources deal with the same subject—use of the English language—each has something different to contribute. They don't all cover the same topics from the same perspective.

Second, "correct" English can be a slippery target in ten shades of gray, so when faced with a usage dilemma, it's a help to hear from more than one authority. If the experts agree, you can feel comfortable following their lead, and when they don't, you can feel comfortable choosing one of several valid options, knowing you're not violating any hard-and-fast rule.

> **Tip**
>
> If you're working with words in a field that uses specialized terminology—law, finance, medicine, real estate, high tech, etc.—be aware that many special-topic, industry-specific dictionaries and other reference sources are available. Having the right one at your elbow can save much time and many queries.

The World Wide Reference Department

In addition to online versions of some of the hard-copy reference tools just listed, the Internet offers a nearly endless supply of editorial guidance. It's also the quickest, easiest way to double-check almost any fact, as long as you remember one thing: *just because it's posted on the Internet doesn't mean it's correct*. Carefully consider the source of any information you find online and try to corroborate it before you use it.

For some sites to consider in starting your own online reference library, see "Online Editorial Resources" at the end of this chapter.

Do It with Style

If we could offer only one bit of editorial advice, it would be this: keep and use a *style sheet*. Really. It's that important.

A style sheet is nothing more—and nothing less—than a listing of anything a writer, editor, or proofreader wants to remember and keep consistent while working through a piece of writing (for a sample, see the "Starter Style Sheet" at the end of this chapter). That includes particular spellings, capitalizations, abbreviations, punctuation, number and formatting conventions, and anything else that's quirky, that crops up repeatedly, or that might be hard to remember. Different things go on style sheets for different reasons.

Some style sheet entries are records of decisions made about items that appear in more than one way in a piece of writing—will it be *catsup* or *ketchup*, OK or *okay*? *Webster's* considers either, um, OK, so it's up to you to settle on one and stick with it.

How to choose? If you're working for a client, and that client has a preference, the client's choice goes on your style sheet and you make sure the term is used that way everywhere it appears.

If there is no client preference, and no other reason to choose one form or the other, you opt for efficiency and choose the one that appears most often. That way, to keep things consistent, you'll need to mark fewer changes overall.

Tip

Sometimes you'll make a style decision, only to reverse it later. If you're working on hard copy, and you know an item can be treated in more than one way, it's often helpful, early on, to note on the style sheet *where* (page number or other locator) the term appears along with the term itself. You might see two or three *OK*s early on, and add the abbreviated form to your style sheet. Then later, you realize the author has shifted to—and stayed with—*okay*. If you've noted the location of those *OK*s, it's quick work to go back and change them to *okay*. If you're working electronically, it's not as important to note the locations—you can always simply do a search for the term you want to change.

Other things go on style sheets because they're unusual or even unique (such as people's names) and may never find their way into *Webster's*. You might be hard-pressed to remember, ten pages after you first see it, that *ESPI* stands for *Electronic Speckle Pattern Interferometry*. But if you enter that acronym and what it stands for on your style sheet when you first see and confirm it, and then refer to the style sheet whenever you see the term again, you'll never let it slip by as *Electronic Speckle Patterned Interferometry*.

What else goes on a style sheet? Lots of things. Spellings for standard English words and terms that appear in your document but that you can't seem to remember no matter how many times you look them up (and we all have those blind spots), how foreign words are handled, how often to spell out acronyms, what information goes in tables, how lists are introduced—there's no such thing as trivia when building a style sheet. It *all* matters, and anything is fair game. If there's any chance you (or the person who comes after you) will wonder about and want to confirm a spelling or some other detail, take a few seconds and note it on your style sheet.

Tip

If you're working electronically, keep your style sheet document open but minimized, so you can add or refer to it quickly. Try to enter words alphabetically, but don't worry if the order is a little off—you can always highlight and alphabetize your list later, in a flash, using your software's sorting function (in Word, go to Table > Sort).

So what *doesn't* go on a style sheet? Normally, unless you need a memory jog, you wouldn't include familiar English words and phrases that appear in *Webster's* or another general-purpose dictionary, or proper names that are well known. *Turtle, Burma,* and *daffodil* probably don't belong on a style sheet. But *terrapin, Myanmar,* and *Narcissus* might.

Tip

If you have lots of information under any one style sheet heading, it's easier to find what you're looking for if you break it down further. For instance, under the heading "Numbers, Dates, and Times," you might have the subheadings "Units of Measure," "Mathematical Operators," and "Years."

Follow the Leader and Pass It Around

There are two reasons to keep a style sheet: to make sure you remember editorial decisions and details and to help others do the same.

If a style sheet already exists for your document, that means someone besides you—maybe the author, maybe a previous editor—has already thought about maintaining consistency as the writing makes its way through other hands. Bravo! Be sure to review any existing style sheet carefully, follow the conventions shown on it, and add to it as you discover new things.

And sometimes the effort to achieve consistency extends to more than just the work in hand. A style sheet can be developed and maintained for a single document, but it can also be created for a client or department or for an entire organization (a *house* style sheet), to keep writing consistent no matter how many wordsmiths are at work. The more tightly focused the style sheet, the more priority you should give it. For instance, in case of conflict, a department style sheet would trump a house style sheet, and a document style sheet would trump both. Be sure to use, add to, and pass on any and all style sheets that pertain to your project.

> **Tip**
>
> If more than one person will work on a piece of writing, let any relevant style sheets travel with it, so everyone who works on it can use the same conventions. If more than one person will add to a style sheet, date each version of the style sheet and ask each person to note his or her entries with a different color or symbol. That way everyone will know what's most current and who has added what.
>
> Even when only one person is building a style sheet, if others will receive updated versions of it, it's very helpful to highlight in the most recent edition what's new since the previous one so the recipient can see changes and additions at a glance.

The Last Word in Style

Keeping and using a style sheet will give you writing that's—from the standpoint of style—98 percent consistent. Here's how to squeeze out that last 2 percent: in addition to a style sheet, keep an informal *search list* as you work.

It's just a fact that no one can note every editorial error or inconsistency when reading something for the first time. For one thing, until you've seen a word, term, or formatting element more than once, and seen it used differently, you can't even know that there *is* inconsistency.

Always, as you work through a document, you'll notice details and think "Oh! Is that correct? Did that appear earlier? How was it handled?" If a decision needs to be made, you make it and add it to the style sheet. But what about those possible earlier occurrences? That's where a search list comes in.

A search list is a set of very informal notes you keep strictly for yourself as an adjunct to the style sheet, a place to jot down words or any other items you want to be sure you go back and verify and correct as needed before you hand off your project.

Whenever you think of something you want to check for consistency, write it on your search list. Then you can keep an eye out for search list items as you do a second reading, or if you're working electronically, you can do separate global searches for each item at the very end (see "Do It in Stages" later in this chapter for a detailed discussion of this process).

It takes very little time to keep and act on a search list, but it's the surest way to know that your document and your style sheet are in perfect agreement.

Make Your Mark

It's almost time to take pen or pencil in hand or scoot up to the keyboard. Here's how to use those tools when you do.

On Hard Copy

Editorial professionals working on hard copy use a special vocabulary of marks to indicate changes in a piece of writing. It's a type of shorthand understood by most people who work with words. You don't *have* to use these marks, as long as you and whoever will interpret them understand the marks you do use, but many people find it convenient to use the standard marks, just because they are so widely understood. To view the entire lexicon, see "Proofreader's Marks" at the end of this chapter.

Editors and proofreaders use the same marks, but because of space constraints, they often use them differently. Most editors place marks within the text itself, because they usually work on double-spaced pages that have not yet been formatted and have the room to do so.

Proofreaders, on the other hand, often read a document late in the editorial process, after the piece has taken its final designed and single-spaced form. For them, there is no room to indicate changes within the text. So proofreaders— and editors, when space is tight—put marks in the margins, with a caret in the text to indicate the location of the change. Here's a bit of hard-copy markup, as both an editor (above) and a proofreader (below) would approach it:

If a change involves adding more text than will fit either between lines or in the margin, you can write it on a separate sheet, label it *A*, insert the sheet imme- diately following the page to which it applies, and indicate with a caret in the text and a note in the margin where the new text should go ("Insert A").

Tip

If you're working on hard copy, you might need to fax your changes to some- one else. If you do, be careful to keep all markings dark (using an erasable pen, not a pencil) and well away from the edges of the page, because fax transmis- sions can cut off margins.

In Electronic Files

Today most writing is done on a computer screen, and most editing is done the same way. The majority of your editing will be done using word processing software, such as Microsoft Word, or using Adobe Acrobat to edit PDF files. Using electronic markup, you never have to worry about squeezing words between two lines, erasing something (in ink!) if you change your mind, or running out of room for new text or a comment.

For example, both Word and Acrobat have reviewing and markup tools that let one or more people insert and delete text and add comments and queries very clearly.

These are great advantages, but there are more: Using electronic editing tools, you can search for every occurrence of a term. And in Word you can also search for a heading level to quickly be sure they all match and numbers are sequential, you can run a spell-checker to catch what your eyes may have missed, you can alphabetize lists with one click, you can record a macro to perform tedious tasks with one keystroke, and much more. (For more on these gifts from the editing gods, see Part Three.)

Electronic editing is not only far more convenient; it can also produce a far cleaner and more consistent result than hard-copy editing. Get to know all the editing tools your software offers; it will be time well spent.

Tip

Before you make a mark, with either pencil or keyboard, be sure you have a clean copy of the original work safely duplicated or saved. And if you're working electronically, be sure to save often (every few minutes) and back up regularly (every few hours) to preserve your hard work.

For backing up your work, you can use external media such as CDs, Memory Sticks, or even a separate external hard drive.

Learn the Art of Asking

As you review almost any piece of writing, you'll find you have questions. In the world of editing, they're called *queries*. Knowing what to ask—and when and how—is a bit of an art, and mastering it can make all the difference between useful answers from happy authors who appreciate your professionalism, and partial answers—or nonanswers—from testy authors you've unwittingly offended or annoyed.

What to Ask and What to Tell

Questions that arise while editing can be about almost anything that seems confusing, incorrect, or inconsistent. "Marseilles, France, or Marseilles, Illinois?" "Don Blake is referred to as the CEO on page 1, but the president on page 4. Which is correct?"

And sometimes you'll want to explain a change to the writer, who might otherwise not see the reason for it: "Change for consistency with earlier usage" or "Per *Webster's*."

Other times you'll want to both explain and query: "I've assumed you mean Marseilles, France, not Marseilles, Illinois. Correct?"

It's not necessary to explain every correction, of course; you can simply change *compliment* to *complement* or *effect* to *affect* with no comment. But you might want to explain why you've made it *the president* instead of *the President* ("Lowercase per department style sheet and *Chicago*"). If you make such a change many times, one explanation—the first time you make the change—is enough.

> **Important:** If you make the same change three times, before making it again, check with the author, another person in a position to know, or an existing style sheet to be sure you're not changing something that should remain the way it appears. If it's not convenient to get an immediate answer, add the item to a list of questions to be resolved before you complete your work (see "Fewer Is Better"). Then, until you get your answer, if you're working on hard copy, keep track of where the item appears.

Choosing Your Words

When it comes to querying, think of yourself as a diplomat with a critical mission on a tight word budget. Focus on being three things—concise, precise, and polite:

- **Use as few words as possible to express your exact meaning.** The author's time, like yours, is at a premium; chattiness is rarely appreciated and can obscure your vital question. Ask "Does this statistic apply to all years or just 2004?" instead of "You know, I'm wondering if this amount is really right for the whole decade. Can you tell me if it is or if it covers only 2004?"

- **Ask for exactly the information you need, leaving no room for ambiguity.** "Should the value be 24, 25, or 26?" will almost always elicit the response you need. "Is 24 correct?" could result in a frustrating "No."
- **Keep the tone of your query unfailingly respectful.** Under no circumstances should you ever seem to criticize or rebuke the writer. "Sloppy transition; please fix" not only antagonizes the writer but also gives him or her little information about what you want. Instead, say "Will readers understand how this point follows from the previous one? Can you clarify?"

Fewer Is Better

As we noted, everyone has limited time. And when it comes to answering questions, people can also have limited patience. When deciding what and how to query, keep those things in mind. Query only the items you can't reasonably resolve on your own, and do it in a way (and at a time) that's most efficient.

Necessary queries fall into two groups:

- Items the author can answer later, while reviewing your work
- Questions best resolved before you complete your work

If a question pertains to just one or a few spots in a piece of writing, it's fine to simply attach individual queries for the author's review.

But if there's a question about something that appears frequently in the work, and the answer might result in many changes, try to resolve it early on.

For example, if the same person's name appears as both Smith and Smithe, and that person is mentioned frequently, try to verify the correct form, with either the author or another trusted authority. A quick phone call or e-mail should clear up the confusion; then you can confidently make any needed changes as you come across each instance, and no one will have to sift through the whole document later to find them all.

If there are several such issues, rather than calling or e-mailing the author with each one, keep a running list and seek answers to all of them at once. The best time is just after you've completed your first reading and before you start your second (see "Do It in Stages" later in this chapter).

Going Global

If it's not possible to get an answer to a pervasive issue before you finish your work, you can use a *global* query. A global query is one that is attached where an inconsistency or possible error first appears but that applies to every instance of the item in the entire work. "Global: Is it Smith or Smithe? Please verify and make consistent throughout."

That's easy enough to ask (maybe *too* easy; make sure you limit such requests to times when you really have no other option), but it might be difficult for the author to do. Should the author be unable to make all the changes, there's one more way to ensure they are made, even after the work leaves your hands. A proofreader who will be doing a final careful check once all the edits have been incorporated can be alerted to any global items still outstanding and make the needed adjustments.

Tip

Often the best way to alert the author and others to global issues is in a cover letter, returned with the finished job. Even if you don't have specific questions or requests, you'll almost always want to let the author know a bit about what you've done and how you've approached the project. A cover letter is the perfect place to do that.

Making Queries Stick

If there's an art to asking editorial questions, there's a craft to actually attaching them to the page. How you do it depends on whether you're working on hard copy or an electronic file.

On Hard Copy. When working on paper, you have two options. If there's room, you can write your query in the page margin. Otherwise, break out some sticky notes, write your message on one, and attach it to the edge of the page, near the item in question. If the note is very lengthy, you can write it on a separate sheet, insert the sheet immediately after the page to which it applies, and direct the reviewer to it in the margin ("See query next page").

It's a good idea to write the page and line number on each note, too, in case the note falls off or is placed incorrectly, and to help the author quickly locate the area in question.

> **T i p**
>
> When writing queries in the margin of a page, it's helpful to differentiate between questions ("Change OK?") and instructions ("bf") by drawing a box around one and a circle around the other:

Come see the sea lions at ⟨PIER⟩ 39. | all caps OK? |

Stressed spelled backwards is desserts! (bf)

In an Electronic File. When working onscreen, you can use your software's comments feature to place queries in the margin, or in boxes when using Adobe Acrobat.

 In Word, you can also insert queries directly into the text, setting them off between characters (such as multiple asterisks or curly braces) that don't appear elsewhere:

 {{Q: 2004 or 2005?}}}

That way a search for the character(s) will quickly turn up all the queries in the document. Ask the person who will answer the queries how he or she would prefer to see them.

Reviewing Your Queries

However you attach queries, be sure to take a few moments at the end of your work to reread them for accuracy, brevity, diplomacy, and typos. Clean, nicely worded queries reflect a respectful, professional attitude and are far more likely to elicit the same in the person who answers them.

Do It in Stages

Just to review: *no one can catch every glitch in a document of any length when first reading it.* We don't care how sharp, experienced, or dedicated you are, it just can't be done. It's in the nature of editing to make discoveries and decisions as the work progresses. As you do, you'll be adding them to your style sheet and search list, then doubling back to verify items in the early part of the project.

So unless you're dealing with a three-line memo, the only way to do a good, thorough editorial review is to do it in stages, with different objectives at each one. If you keep your focus on just one or a few things at a time, you're far less likely to be distracted or to overlook details.

The stages that follow outline a general approach to any editorial project; for a more detailed approach tailored specifically to proofreading, see the "Professional 8-Stage Proofreading Checklist" in Appendix B.

The Preliminary Skim

Before you begin marking, look quickly through the document to get an overall sense of it. How long is it? Are all the parts there? Does it seem generally well constructed, or will it need lots of help? Will you need to use any special reference materials as you work? Are there many tables, lots of formulas, numerous illustrations?

This preliminary assessment will help you understand the amount and level of work required, how best to budget your time, what additional materials, if any, you'll need, and whether you'll be able to complete the project in the time allotted.

The First Pass

Once you have a feel for the project, start reading the document at the beginning, character by character, word by word, and line by line. As you go, watch for anything amiss—incorrect spelling, grammar, punctuation, or usage; headings that don't match the text that follows; references to illustrations that don't exist; numbers out of sequence; italics that are misplaced or missing; anything and everything that might confuse readers or distract them, for even a fraction of a second, from the author's message.

If you're working above the level of proofreading, be on the lookout, too, as appropriate, for errors of fact or in logic, faulty transitions, awkward wordings, or ineffective presentation. (For more on what to look for as you work, see Part Two.)

Keep in mind the golden rule of editing and proofreading: *Never assume*. If there's the slightest doubt about any item, always check and verify it.

This first pass is where most of the editorial work gets done and is the slowest going, as you correct, reword, query, consult references, and develop your style sheet.

Tip

Just as a style sheet can help you keep track of conventions, a checklist can help you remember to look at all the right things as you edit. For a collection of reliable reminders, see the checklists in Part Two and Appendix B.

The Second Pass

With your style sheet complete and as many global queries answered as possible, read through the entire document a second time, looking for anything you might have missed on the first pass and making any needed alterations to ensure consistency and accuracy. If you're working onscreen, it's often helpful at this stage to read the material without the markup visible (for more on that, see Chapter 6). That way you'll see the results of your first-pass edits more clearly.

Don't expect this pass to be swift; although you won't be marking as much as you did on the first pass, you'll need to read the material just as carefully.

The Final (Short) Passes

At the end of the second pass, your search list will probably still contain several small items you want to verify—spellings, heading styles and wordings, numerical sequences, and anything else you want to be certain is correct and consistent. The best way to be sure you've found each item and brought it into line is to search separately and sequentially through the whole document for each item, one at a time. (Naturally, global searches for individual words or phrases are easiest to do when working on an electronic file.)

This one-thing-at-a-time approach will also help you ensure the highest level of accuracy and consistency in other elements of the project, too. At this final stage, look separately at such things as:

- Section numbers and titles
- Text headings
- Lists and tables
- Captions and labels
- Page numbers, headers, and footers
- Table of contents entries

Looking for specific search-list items or at particular project elements individually won't take long, and you'll be surprised at what you pick up on these final brief passes that you didn't see when you were deciding whether a pronoun was correct or a verb was in the right tense.

And finally, if you're using word processing software such as Word, the *very* last pass is the spell-check. It's not infallible, but it's easy to run, and it's another set of (electronic) eyes. Every typo a spell-checker catches is one more a reader will never see. (Unfortunately, as of this writing, Adobe Acrobat would check the spelling only in the comments inserted in a PDF document, not in the actual text of the document.)

> **T i p**
>
> In addition to a spell-check at the end of your work, do a search for double spaces. Although a single space is considered correct these days, many writers still tap the space bar twice after a period or a colon. And extra spaces are very easy to insert or overlook while editing. Fortunately, they're also easy to delete once you've found them.

Tools

These are the proofreader's marks used by editorial professionals and lots of other people, too, to indicate desired changes in writing that's on hard copy.

Proofreader's Marks

Explanation	Mark in margin	Mark in copy	Corrected copy
delete	ℛ	the careful /reader	the careful reader
close up space	⌢	the careful r͡eader	the careful reader
delete and close up space	ℛ̂	the careful r̸eader	the careful reader
lowercase	⒧Ⓒ	⎸he careful reader	the careful reader
italic type	Ⓘⓣⓐⓛ	the _careful_ reader	the *careful* reader
roman type	ⓡⓞⓜ	the⟨careful⟩reader	the careful reader
boldface type	ⓑⓕ	the careful reader	the **careful** reader
small capital letters	ⓈⒸ	The Careful Reader	THE CAREFUL READER
capital	ⓒⓐⓟ	the careful reader	The careful reader
subscript	⌄2	H2O	H$_2$O
superscript	2⌄	the careful reader2	the careful reader^2

continued

Explanation	Mark in margin	Mark in copy	Corrected copy
transpose	(tr)	the craeful reader	the careful reader
let it stand; disregard previous correction	(stet)	the ~~careful~~ reader	the careful reader
spell out	(sp)	②careful readers	two careful readers
insert space	(#)	thecareful reader	the careful reader
insert period	⊙	The careful reader‸	The careful reader.
insert comma	⋀	the careful‸attentive reader	the careful, attentive reader
insert semicolon	⋀	the careful reader‸the thoughtful reader	the careful reader; the thoughtful reader
insert colon	⊙	the careful reader‸	the careful reader:
insert apostrophe	⋁	the careful readers guide	the careful reader's guide
insert quotation marks	⋁ / ⋁	⌄the careful reader⌄	"the careful reader"
insert character	a	the creful reader	the careful reader
insert word	*careful*	the‸reader	the careful reader
insert slash (virgule)	⫽	the careful reader‸	the careful reader/
insert parentheses	{ / }	the‸careful‸reader	the (careful) reader
en dash	$\frac{1}{N}$	1948-)955	1948–1955
1-em dash	$\frac{1}{M}$	Reading carefully--not something everyone can do.	Reading carefully—not something everyone can do.
hyphen	= / =	Read word‸for‸word.	Read word-for-word.
begin paragraph	(¶)	Do you know any careful readers?|We need one as soon as possible.	Do you know any careful readers? We need one as soon as possible.
run in	(run in)	Do you know any careful readers?⏜ We need one.	Do you know any careful readers? We need one.
align	‖	‖the careful ‖reader	the careful reader
	(align)	‖the careful ‖reader	the careful reader
move down	⏜	[the c⌐a⌐reful reader	the careful reader

Explanation	Mark in margin	Mark in copy	Corrected copy
move up	⌐	⌊ the c⌐areful reader	the careful reader
center	][	] the careful reader [	the careful reader
equal spacing	(eq #)	the˄careful˄reader	the careful reader
begin new line	⌐	Reading carefully is something not⌐every person can do.	Reading carefully is something not every person can do.
wrong font	(wf)	the careful (reader)	the careful reader

Starter Style Sheet

The typical style sheet that follows has space for the editorial detail and decisions you're most likely to want to record. To give you an idea of what to include, we've shown some sample entries. But remember, they're only examples. Your customized style sheet should include information specific to *your* project, client or department, or organization.

For a style sheet with space for all the detail the pickiest editorial professional might desire, see the "Expanded/Professional Style Sheet Template" in Appendix B.

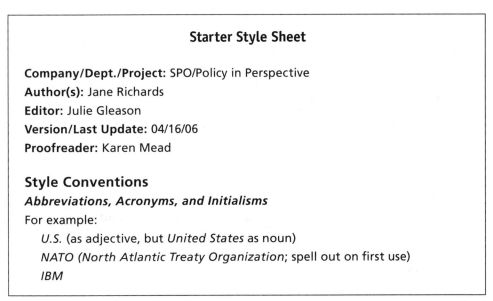

Starter Style Sheet

Company/Dept./Project: SPO/Policy in Perspective
Author(s): Jane Richards
Editor: Julie Gleason
Version/Last Update: 04/16/06
Proofreader: Karen Mead

Style Conventions
Abbreviations, Acronyms, and Initialisms
For example:

U.S. (as adjective, but *United States* as noun)
NATO (North Atlantic Treaty Organization; spell out on first use)
IBM

continued

Headings

For example:

Lowercase articles (*a, an, the*), the conjunctions *and, but, for, or,* and *nor,* and prepositions with fewer than five letters (*in, to,* but *Neither, Through, Between*), unless they begin or end a heading (*A Curious Run-In*)

Capitalize first letter of each word (except those noted above) in a compound (*High-Density, Up-to-Date*)

14-point Times bold, flush left, for all first-level subheads

Lists and Tables

For example:

Start each list item with a bullet and a capital letter

End each list item with a period unless no item in list is a complete sentence

Use bold for left-column table entries

Numbers, Dates, and Times

For example:

Spell out one through ten, use numerals for 11 and up, but always use numerals with percentages (*3 percent*) and abbreviated units of measure (*1 km, 3 MB, 64K*)

1990s, not *1990's*

7 a.m.

Punctuation

For example:

Use series comma (*A, B, and C;* not *A, B and C*)

No space around em dashes—like this

Use en dash in ranges (*1999–2004; M–F*)

Other Conventions

For example:

Italicize foreign words not in *Webster's*

Capitalize first letter of each word in department names (*Customer Care Department*)

For onscreen labels, use capitalization as shown onscreen (*Save As, File name*)

Words and Terms

For example:

adviser (not advisor)	nonnuclear
bimonthly	online
decision making (n)	point-of-sale (POS) advertising
disc (compact disc)	POS (point of sale)
disk (computer disk)	Post-it® (symbol in promo
e-mail	materials only)
every day (adv; "I run every day")	real time (n)
everyday (adj; "everyday event")	real-time (adj)
hand off (v)	recreate, but re-create (create again)
hand-off (n)	reengineering
Internet	self-correcting
intranet	Web (the Web)
multilevel (adj)	web site (contrary to *Webster's*)

Online Editorial Resources

When you're working with words, you'll have questions. Find answers to many of them, quickly and easily, at the Web sites that follow. (**Note:** The information here was current at the time of this writing, but on the Web change is the only constant. Be prepared to do a little detective work should any of these addresses change.)

1. **Acronym Finder (acronymfinder.com).** Find definitions in seconds for almost any acronym, abbreviation, or initialism. A terrific tool; lets you sort by category and industry.

2. **Answers.com (answers.com).** If you have questions, Answers.com has up-to-date answers. It's like an encyclopedia crossed with a dictionary crossed with Google.

3. **AP Stylebook (apstylebook.com).** The journalist's standard style guide is available online by subscription for $20 per year. With a site license, you can also customize it with your own entries.

4. **Bartleby.com (bartleby.com).** This is your dream library, online. From reference books to poetry to fiction to the classics, this site has the books—and the search tools. Look up facts, nail down quotations, or read a whole book, right here.

5. *The Chicago Manual of Style*, 15th edition (**chicagomanualofstyle.org/ search.html**). This search tool speeds you to answers in the print version of the editor's standard style guide.

6. **Google (google.com).** How are others using a term or spelling a name? This giant database will tell you. But remember—it simply contains what's published, mistakes and all. If you can, make sure several Google sources agree before you use what you find.

7. **Guide to Grammar & Writing (grammar.ccc.commnet.edu/grammar).** This site will fill you in, good-naturedly, on anything you'd like to know about grammar and composition. Nicely indexed and easy to use.

8. **Merriam-Webster Online (m-w.com).** If you can't spell a word, how do you look it up? Answer: Go to this site. All of *Merriam-Webster's Collegiate Dictionary* is here, plus search options that steer you to correct spellings, and more. You can use the tenth edition at no charge or subscribe to use the eleventh edition. And if you already own the hard copy of the eleventh, a year's subscription is free.

9. **Thesaurus.com (thesaurus.reference.com).** Have your way with words. This is your online look-up tool for synonyms and antonyms.

10. **Webopedia.com (webopedia.com).** A great source for computer and Internet technology terms and definitions.

11. **yourDictionary.com (yourdictionary.com).** How do you say hello in Hindi? Find out here. This site links to online dictionaries that translate English into more than three hundred languages and vice versa. It has a world of information on English words, too.

PART TWO

The 3 Cs: What to Look for as You Work

Effective writing needs to be three things—*correct, consistent,* and *clear.* In this part, we'll show you what that means and give you the tools to ensure that anything you edit is all three. For those with loftier goals, we'll also give guidance on how to take writing to the next level—*compelling.*

3

Is It Correct?

At the risk of echoing a former president, the answer depends on what you mean by *correct*.

For most editors and proofreaders, *correct* doesn't mean "true." It's usually someone else's job (the author's, for instance) to vouch for the veracity of the content. It *might* be your job to check facts, and you're certainly free to flag something you know to be false, but in most cases *editorial* correctness is a whole different topic.

From an editorial standpoint, correctness has to do with whether the right caption goes with the right picture, whether numbered items are sequential, whether heading levels are accurate, whether bullet styles are consistent, and many other details.

And, of course, mostly it has to do with the mechanics of the writing—spelling, grammar, capitalization, punctuation, and so forth. It has to do with all those language things you learned (or were exposed to) in school. Is it *which* or *that*? *Who* or *whom*? *Its* or *it's*? It's (not *its*) an editor's job to know the answers.

But let's face it: for most people, English class is a dim memory. You know writing has its rules, but you're a little hazy on a few of them.

What's more, "correct" English is a moving target; both the language and the rules evolve over time. And despite what Ms. Stickler told you in eighth grade, some of the "rules" were never rules at all. So deciding what's currently correct can tax the best of us, even the pros.

Here's help. In this chapter, you'll find mercifully simple answers to the preceding questions and many more. We've chosen the writing dilemmas that seem to stymie most people most often and provided just what you need to solve them, briefly. We know you *mean* to read that stack of English usage manuals, cover to cover, but until you get to them, here are the highlights.

And you don't even need to take notes. At the end of the chapter, you'll find tools to help you remember it all.

The Pieces of the Puzzle

A sentence is like a jigsaw puzzle, and the parts of speech are its pieces. When the pieces fit, the picture they form is clear, even beautiful. The pieces are the same ones you met in Ms. Stickler's class, so they're probably old acquaintances. But in case it's been a while, here's a quick refresher before we move on:

- **Noun**—a word that indicates a person, place, thing, or idea. Proper nouns represent unique, named people or things and always start with a capital letter (*Mike, London*). Common nouns indicate one or more of a whole group of things, and unless they begin a sentence, they start with a lowercase letter (*tree, freedom*).
- **Pronoun**—a word that stands in for a noun (*I, he, them, who, that, which, all, anyone, one, none,* etc.).
- **Adjective**—a word that describes a noun (*small* woman, *tall* man, *windy* day).
- **Verb**—a word that shows action (*walk, read, go, speak*) or a state of being (*be, seem, feel, become*).
- **Adverb**—a word that describes a verb (walk *quickly*, read *slowly*), another adverb (walk *very* quickly, read *quite* slowly), or an adjective (a *very* small woman, a *remarkably* tall man).
- **Conjunction**—a word that connects other words or parts of a sentence (*and, or, but, since, because,* etc.).
- **Preposition**—a word that "positions" other words in a sentence (*about, above, between, in, on, out, to, up,* etc.).

> **Note:** With each of the topics in this chapter, we've included references to some well-respected resources for further reading. We bow to their wisdom and expertise. *CMS* is *The Chicago Manual of Style*, 15th edition; *Garner* is *Garner's Modern American Usage*, by Bryan A. Garner; *Woe* is *Woe Is I*, by Patricia T. O'Conner; and *WC* is *Word Court*, by Barbara Wallraff.

The Rules of the Game

To be fair, most of what your English teacher had to tell you was right on.

Now, as then, you really do need to keep your subject and verb on speaking terms; you really do need a semicolon in a sentence like this one.

But a few things have changed in recent years, and a few things were never more than myths. So in the sections that follow, we'll jog your memory on the bedrock basics of grammar and usage, bring you up to date on a few others, and banish some grammar ghosts that have been in the attic far too long.

> **T i p**
>
> Why all the rules? Not because editors are control fiends, although some authors think so. We have standards for writing for the same reason we have rules of the road: so everyone reads the signs and symbols the same way, and no one collides with a comma on the way to clear understanding. Rules serve the reader, which is why editors heed them.

Agreement Is All-Important

Sentences in which the parts don't match up can confuse the reader or alter the meaning. Fortunately, most people naturally choose the right words. But there are times when the right choice is less obvious. Here are the basics of agreement, plus some help with perennial puzzlers.

Counting Is Key. Agreement in *number* is fundamental to good grammar. Singular subjects need singular verbs and singular pronouns, and plural subjects need plural verbs and plural pronouns (*CMS* 5.12, 5.40–41, 5.123).

Correct: *Joe **is a man** who **knows his** own mind.*

Correct: *Bob and Steve **are men** who **know their** own minds.*

Simple enough. But what happens when more words move in? To keep your subject and verb in sync, don't be distracted by what comes between them (*CMS* 5.123; *Garner* 174–75; *WC* 92–93; *Woe* 50–53).

Correct: ***Each** of the candidates **has her** strengths.*

Incorrect: ***Each** of the candidates **have their** strengths.*

And make sure you've matched the right subject with the right verb. Watch out for sentences that have more than one.

Correct: *She is one of those people **who make** it look easy.*

Incorrect: *She is one of those people **who makes** it look easy.*

In this sentence, the first subject is *she*, and the first verb is *is*. No confusion there. But here's the tricky part: The second subject is *who*, and the second verb is *make*. And because *who* is standing in for *people*, it needs a plural verb (*make*, not *makes*).

> **Tip**
> With the phrases *one of the*, *one of those*, or *one of these*, look for the pronoun *that* or *who* before the verb. If it's there, the verb that follows is plural. If it's not, the verb is singular (*Garner* 572–73; *Woe* 60–61).

Sometimes subjects come in more than one part. When they do, here's how to decide whether to use a singular or plural verb (*Woe* 52–53).

With *or* or *nor*, if both parts of the subject are singular, use a singular verb.

Correct: *Either blue or black **is** acceptable.*

Incorrect: *Either blue or black **are** acceptable.*

If they're both plural, use a plural verb.

Correct: *Neither the sandwiches nor the doughnuts **were** eaten.*

Incorrect: *Neither the sandwiches nor the doughnuts **was** eaten.*

If one part of the subject is singular, and one part is plural, match the verb to the part closest to it.

Correct: *Neither the sandwiches nor the doughnut **was** eaten.*

Correct: *Neither the sandwich nor the doughnuts **were** eaten.*

And sometimes a subject can be either singular *or* plural. When the subject is a word that indicates a group—like *majority, couple, number, all, any,* or *none*—the verb form you choose depends on what you mean. Are you talking about the group as a whole or its individual members (*CMS* 5.8; *WC* 122–31; *Woe* 25–28, 53)?

Correct: *The couple* next door *has two cats.*

Correct: *A couple* of offers *have just come in.*

Correct: *The majority* **wants** *change.*

Correct: *A majority* of the members **want** *a new policy.*

> ### Tip
> There's no substitute for thinking it through, but with subjects like these, *the* often points to a singular meaning, while *a* (especially with *of . . .*) points to the plural.

Timing Is Everything. While verbs are busy agreeing with their subjects, they must also keep an eye on the clock. The form of the verb shows the tense, or the "when," of the action—the past, the present, or the future, and different divisions of each. When the same time frame applies to all parts of the sentence, it's not hard to pick the right verbs (*CMS* 5.115–21; *Garner* 777–79; *Woe* 730).

Correct: *Every morning she* **runs** *(present),* **takes** *(present) a shower, and* **eats** *(present) breakfast.*

Correct: *Every morning she* **ran** *(past),* **took** *(past) a shower, and* **ate** *(past) breakfast.*

But it gets a little trickier when time zones overlap. When something started in the past and continues to the present, take care not to cut off the action too soon.

Correct: *I **have gone*** (present perfect) *there for two years.* (And I still go there.)

Correct: *I **went*** (past) *there for two years.* (But I no longer do.)

Correct: *I **haven't done*** (present perfect) *it yet.* (But I still might.)

Incorrect: *I **didn't do*** (past) *it yet.* (Time for action is all in the past; conflicts with *yet*, which implies it might still happen.)

And when a sentence starts in one time zone and ends in another, watch to be sure the verbs follow suit.

Correct: *If Harry **says*** (present) *so, I **will believe*** (future) *it.*

Correct: *If Harry **said*** (past) *so, I **would believe*** (conditional) *it.*

Incorrect: *If Harry **said*** (past) *so, I **will believe*** (future) *it.*

> ### Tip
> When the verb in the first part of an "if" sentence is in the present tense, the verb in the second part starts with *will* (future). When the verb in the first part is in the past tense, the verb in the second part starts with *would* (conditional) (*Woe* 75–77).

Me, Myself, and I. Is it *he* or *him*, *me* or *I*, *she* or *her*? The answer depends on just one thing—is it a subject or an object (*CMS* 5.40–42, 5.47; *Garner* 642–44; *WC* 132–36; *Woe* 10–13)?

A subject is the one *doing* the action.

Correct: *Jim called Susan.*

Correct: *He called Susan.*

An object is the *receiver* of the action.

Correct: *Jim called **Susan.***

Correct: *Jim called **her.***

It's also what's being "positioned" by a preposition (in this case, *between*).

Correct: *The call was between **Jim** and **Susan.***

Correct: *The call was between **him** and **her.***

Incorrect: *The call was between **he** and **she.***

To choose the right personal pronoun, first decide whether you need a subject or an object; then choose the one that fits.

Subject Pronouns	**Object Pronouns**
I, we	me, us
you	you
he, she, it, they	him, her, it, them

> **Tip**
>
> When you see a preposition before a pronoun, it's a tip-off you need the object form (*the fog rolled **over them***).

Pronouns that include *self* or *selves* (*myself, ourselves, yourself, yourselves,* etc.) are just for emphasis or to toss the focus back to the subject. They should never be used in place of a subject or an object.

Correct: *I said I'd do it **myself.***

Correct: *He **himself** already knew that.*

Incorrect: *Three others and **myself** (make it **I**) will attend.*

Incorrect: *The group will include John, Henry, and **myself** (make it **me**).*

Apostrophes Are for Possessives, Not Plurals

We've all seen the signs and read the ads: *The Wallace's. Hundreds of Overstock's. Only Three Day's Left.* Not one of those apostrophes belongs, but they show up so often that they've almost stopped looking like gate-crashers.

Just Say No. When adding *s* to any word, it's tempting for writers to tuck in an apostrophe. Sometimes their fingers do it before their minds can weigh in. So keep that on *your* mind as you edit, and remember:

To make most singular words plural, use the *s* alone, with no apostrophe.

Correct: *We invited Jim and Susan (the Smiths) to join us.*

Incorrect: *We invited Jim and Susan (the Smith's) to join us.*

Correct: *We have a lot full of new Toyotas.*

Incorrect: *We have a lot full of new Toyota's.*

If the word ends in *ch, j, s, sh, x,* or *z,* add an *es*—again, with no apostrophe (*CMS* 7.6).

Correct: *The membership at both churches is roughly the same.*

To make a singular word show ownership (possessive), add an apostrophe and an *s.* Add the extra *s* even if the word already ends in one (*CMS* 7.17–18).

Correct: *May I give you Chris's voice mail?*

Incorrect: *May I give you Chris' voice mail?*

To make a plural word that already ends in *s* possessive, just add an apostrophe following the *s.* If the plural word ends in something other than *s,* add an apostrophe and an *s,* just as you would for the singular.

Correct: *The Smiths' new car is a Hummer.*

Correct: *The children's favorite pastime is Nintendo.*

Capitals Can Clutter

Ah, those eye-catching capitals. With just a pinky on the Shift key, you can confer importance, singularity, and distinction. You can show and command respect. You can set a word *apart*. So, naturally, many writers are quick to capitalize perfectly ordinary words like *City*, *Company*, *President*, and *Sale*, even when they aren't part of a proper name. Sometimes it seems improper *not* to.

But it's a misuse of power and a mark of misunderstanding to be too free with capitals. Far fewer English words require capitalization than most people think. There are places where capitals belong and places where they don't (*CMS* 8.4–210, 15.4–7, 15.71–76; *Garner* 128–30).

> **Tip**
>
> Some English words are capitalized for logical reasons, and some are capitalized just because. The conventions are based part on reason, part on habit, so it's not always easy to know when to go uppercase and when to stay low. The guidelines here will help you make many decisions, but as you work, keep a good style guide and dictionary close by for further guidance—you'll need them. Rely, too, on any style guidelines you've been given, because certain industries and professions use capitals in their own ways.

When Capitals Are Correct. Use the Shift key for the first letter of:

- The proper names of unique, individual beings, regions, or things

  Correct: *Monday,* *Jane* *leaves for the* *Pacific Northwest.*

- Titles used before a name, as a part of it

  Correct: *I'll refer that question to* *President* *Thomas.*

- Adjectives derived from personal names

  Correct: *She's a fan of* *Victorian* *architecture.*

Use all capitals—with no periods, unless confusion is possible—in abbreviations formed from the first letters of the words in a term.

Correct: *Your appointment is with David M. Sanders,* **MD.**

Correct: *The U.S. military is currently on high alert.* (Periods to prevent misreading *U.S.* as an emphatic form of *us*)

When Capitals Aren't Called For. Use *all* lowercase for:

- Abbreviations of units of measure—*with* periods for English units, *without* them for metric

  Correct: *The room is 13* ***ft.*** *6* ***in.*** *by 12* ***ft.*** *6* ***in.****, or roughly 4* ***m*** *square.*

- Generic terms not part of a proper name

  Correct: *The* **university** *and the* **city** *share resources.*

- Academic subjects and degrees

  Correct: *My* ***bachelor's*** *degree is in* ***history****; my* ***master's*** *is in* ***business administration.***

- Titles of offices (even really important ones) alone or after a name

  Correct: *At that time, Lincoln was the* ***president*** *of the United States.*

- Adjectives derived from proper names but not used literally

  Correct: *Few* ***manila*** *envelopes come from Manila.*

- Names of the seasons

  Correct: *I'll see you this* ***fall*** *or maybe next* ***spring.***

- The compass directions

  Correct: *They live in the* ***South****, so I drive* ***south*** *to see them.*

Capitals in Titles. People tend to get skittish when capitalizing words in titles. They're not sure just what to do. Some people decide based on length: long words get a capital; short words don't. Some people reserve the capital treatment for "important" words. Some egalitarian souls just capitalize everything.

Such chaos isn't necessary. There really are guidelines for capitalizing titles, even if some are at least as arbitrary as any ad hoc system just described. The following rules should put you on firmer ground (*CMS* 8.164–73; *Garner* 129).

Always capitalize the first and last words in a title, regardless of their parts of speech. Elsewhere:

- Capitalize *all* nouns, pronouns (including tiny *it*), verbs (including little *is*), adjectives, and adverbs.
- Capitalize *that* wherever it appears.
- Lowercase the articles *a*, *an*, and *the*.
- Lowercase the conjunctions *and*, *but*, *for*, *or*, and *nor*.
- Capitalize all other conjunctions, such as *since* and *because*.
- Lowercase *as* and *to* wherever they appear.
- Lowercase prepositions with fewer than five letters (like *in*, *out*, *over*, *on*).
- Capitalize prepositions of five letters or more (like *between* and *through*).
- Capitalize the first letter following a colon and, optionally, the first letter following a hyphen or a dash.

Tip

When choosing what to capitalize in a title, remember that the same word isn't always the same part of speech. For instance, *down* is often a preposition, as in *Roll down the Hill*. It's indicating direction, like a proper preposition.

But in *Track Down Your Ancestors*, *down* is an adverb, modifying the verb *track*. So in this case it gets capitalized.

If you've checked a dictionary and you're still not sure of a word's part of speech, *The Chicago Manual of Style* suggests you read it out loud. If you would stress it, capitalize it. If you wouldn't, don't. Frankly, we don't consider that a lot of help. We have a better suggestion: in a pinch, go ahead and capitalize any words in titles that are ordinarily prepositions if they look odd to you lowercase.

Commas Are Crucial

The comma's main job is to prevent confusion. There are times when it's vital, times when it's optional, and times when it's just the wrong choice.

Do use a comma between items in a list, including the last two, when *and* or *or* joins the last item. This is called a *series* (or *serial*) comma, and some writers omit it, particularly those who go by *AP* style. In most cases, though, it's a service to the reader to use it. Here's why (*CMS* 6.19, 6.60; *Garner* 654, 660; *Woe* 137, 139):

> **Correct:** *He called his colleagues, the vice president, and the secretary.*
> (Several phone calls)

> **Incorrect (for same meaning):** *He called his colleagues, the vice president and the secretary.* (Just two phone calls)

Note: When list items have punctuation of their own, separate them with semicolons instead of commas (for more on semicolons, see "Semicolons Are Sophisticated," later in the chapter).

> **Correct:** *The score was Henry, 4; Jeff, 6; and Alan, 12.*

> **Incorrect:** *The score was Henry, 4, Jeff, 6, and Alan, 12.*

> ***Don't*** use a comma when an ampersand replaces the word *and* (*CMS* 6.24).

> **Correct:** *Smith, Jones & Blake is the best firm for the job.*

> **Incorrect:** *Smith, Jones, & Blake is the best firm for the job.*

> ***Do*** use commas between adjectives if you could use *and* between them without affecting the meaning (*CMS* 6.19, 6.39; *Garner* 655).

> **Correct:** *It was a **long, rewarding** discussion.*

> ***Don't*** use commas when a noun and its immediate modifier express a single idea and you couldn't use *and* to join the adjectives (*CMS* 6.39; *Garner* 655).

Correct: *Their office is in an **old brick building**.*

Do use a comma where you want a natural pause (*CMS* 6.29; *Woe* 138).

Correct: *Yes, that seems right to me.*

Correct: *Alternatively, we could ask them to come here.*

Don't use a comma between an introductory phrase and the verb it modifies (*CMS* 6.26; *Garner* 655).

Correct: *Right behind her came the rest.*

Incorrect: *Right behind her, came the rest.*

Do use a comma when two parts of a sentence each have their own subject and verb and there's a word like *and*, *but*, or *or* between them (*CMS* 6.32).

Correct: ***Mark did** the research, and **Tom designed** the site.*

Incorrect: ***Mark did** the research and **Tom designed** the site.*

Don't use a comma when two or more verbs have the same subject, unless misreading is possible or a pause will aid comprehension (*CMS* 6.34).

Correct: *He **walked** to the store and **rode** the bus home.*

Correct: *She **realized** he was the man who had called, and **shouted** his name.*

Comma optional: *He **walked** to the store, and **rode** the bus home.*

Do use commas around extra, nonessential information (*CMS* 6.43; *Garner* 782–83; *WC* 112–17; *Woe* 3, 138).

Correct: *Her husband, Bob, was there.* (She has only one husband.)

Incorrect (unless she's a polygamist): *Her husband Bob was there.*

Don't use commas around information that's necessary to the meaning (*CMS* 6.43; *Garner* 782–83; *WC* 112–17; *Woe* 3, 138).

Correct: *Her brother Bill planned to meet us.* (She has more than one brother.)

Incorrect (if there's more than one brother): *Her brother, Bill, planned to meet us.*

Do use commas around elements of an address or place name (*CMS* 6.47; *Garner* 655).

Correct: *We sent it to Fairfield, Maine, instead of Fairfield, Connecticut.*

Incorrect: *We sent it to Fairfield, Maine instead of Fairfield, Connecticut.*

Do use a comma to set off introductory phrases unless they're very short and no pause is needed (*CMS* 6.25; *Garner* 655; *Woe* 138).

Correct: *As soon as we're done with this topic, we'll tackle the next.*

Comma optional: *On Monday, we'll look at the numbers.*

Comma optional: *Oh, no!*

Don't insert a comma between months and years when they're used without a day or date (*CMS* 6.46; *Garner* 655).

Correct: *The book came out in June 2005.*

Incorrect: *The book came out in June, 2005.*

Commas are **optional** in names that contain *Jr., Sr., II, III, Inc., Ltd.,* etc. If you do use them, use them in pairs (*CMS* 6.49–50; *Garner* 538).

Correct: *James Rogers **Jr.** has been CEO of Rogers **Inc.** since July.*

Also correct: *James Rogers, **Jr.,** has been CEO of Rogers, **Inc.,** since July.*

Conjunctions Can Open; Prepositions Can Close

You might be surprised—and relieved—to know you can stop feeling guilty every time you end a sentence with *on*. Or start one with *but*. The "rule" that sentences mustn't end with a preposition has never been anything but hearsay. Neither has the "rule" that they mustn't start with a conjunction. Both constructions have appeared in proper written English for centuries, because they give it strength, emphasis, and natural phrasing. So go ahead. On these points, defy your English teacher (*CMS* 5.169, 5.191; *Garner* 762, 763; *WC* 105–7; *Woe* 182–83, 185).

Correct: *That jet is the plane he came **in on**.*

Correct: ***But** he left on a single-engine puddle jumper.*

Hyphens Are Helpful (but Not Always Right)

Hyphens, like commas, help keep meanings clear. But they're also a pretty trend-conscious crowd, and the trend is toward fewer, not more.

Not so long ago, prefixes like *un* and *non* sported hyphens the way men once sported fedoras. Now the look is sleek and modern: the hyphens are gone, in most cases, and prefixes ride firmly attached to their words.

The same pattern follows with multiword terms—they often start open, then sprout a hyphen, and finally merge. Consider, in just a few years, the journey from *on line* to *on-line* to *online*. Or the migration in some quarters of *health care* to *healthcare*, without the stop for a hyphen.

To keep current on hyphens, it's best to check the latest style guides and dictionaries. We've done that, and here are the up-to-the-minute results (*CMS* 7.82–90; *Garner* 657–58, 809; *Woe* 145–51). Rely on them for now, but stay tuned.

Do use hyphens:

- *Before* a noun, with two or more words that describe it, when either of the words wouldn't make sense if used there alone (*a well-traveled road, a strong-willed man*)
- Where misreading is possible (*re-creation* vs. *recreation, small-business owner* vs. *small business owner*)
- With prefixes, to separate two *i*'s or two *a*'s (*anti-intellectual, ultra-allergic*)

- With *self* and *ex* (*self-confident, ex-president*)
- With fractions (*three-quarters, two-thirds*—but for words with *half*, check a dictionary)
- In two-word numbers from twenty-one through ninety-nine, when spelled out (*thirty-five, sixty-three*)
- In most terms that have three or more parts (*mother-in-law, two-year-old*)
- In terms that are hyphenated as nouns or adjectives but open as verbs (*a prompt follow-up, a follow-up report,* but *I'll follow up on that*)
- In terms that are hyphenated as adjectives but open as nouns (*decision-making process,* but *he's in charge of decision making*)
- With space following, to stand in for the part of a word shared by another nearby (*both over- and underused*)
- To break a word at the end of a line to make the right margin more even

Tip

In these days of electronic word processing, you see fewer hyphens at the end of lines. By default, Microsoft Word breaks lines only after whole words. But if you or your client prefers tighter, more even margins, you may find yourself reviewing end-of-line word breaks. If so, be sure the hyphen is inserted at the right place in the word. If you have the slightest doubt, verify the syllable divisions in a dictionary and remember that some words break in different places, depending on their meaning: *pro-ject* is to plan for the future; *proj-ect* is a specific job or undertaking.

Don't use hyphens:

- In most two-word descriptors that come *after* the thing they describe, even if the dictionary shows only the hyphenated form (*the road is well traveled, the man is strong willed*)
- In two-word descriptors that come *before* nouns, if either word would make sense used alone or there's no risk of confusion without a hyphen (*clever young woman, employee review form*)
- With adverbs that end in *ly* (*slightly used car, highly skilled executive*)

- In terms that are open as adverbs but hyphenated as adjectives (*the file was brought up to date, the decision was made on the fly,* but *an up-to-date file, an on-the-fly decision*)
- With *very* (*a much-needed friend,* but *a very much needed friend, a very long day*)
- With *least, most,* and *less* (*least likely outcome, most valued effort, less seen species*)

Dashes Are Indispensable

Everybody knows the hyphen, that tiny line that ties words together or, sometimes, splits them apart. And you've no doubt encountered the hyphen's big siblings, the *em dash* and the *en dash.* Here's a quick reminder of which dash to use when (*CMS* 6.83–94; *Garner* 656–57):

The Em Dash (—). If there's a generic dash, this is it. Officially, an em dash is the width of a capital *M* in whatever typeface you're using, and it's a big, bold mark. It signals breaking news—a whole new thought, more information, or an explanation.

If you're using just one em dash, not two, be sure what's set off by the dash ends with a period (or other ending punctuation). A comma won't do. If what's set off falls in the middle of a sentence, surround it on both sides with dashes.

Correct: *It was the best news imaginable—the house was undamaged.*

Incorrect: *Work continued—although slowly, through the night.*

Correct: *Work continued—although slowly—through the night.*

> **Tip**
> Em dashes grab the eye and make a point more pointed, but like any strong punctuation, they're best used sparingly. To avoid confusing the reader, no sentence should contain more than two.

The En Dash (–). Once upon a time, this dash was the width of a capital *N* (hence the name). Now, in the era of word processing, it's officially half the width of an em dash. It's the right punctuation:

- In ranges, in place of the word *to*

  Correct: *We looked all day for the 2001–2002 files.*

  Correct: *Last quarter, January–March, was a real surprise.*

  Correct: *The Cleveland–Toronto flight has been delayed.*

  But use the word *to* or *through*, not an en dash, if you use the word *from*, and use *and* if you use the word *between*.

  Correct: *Last quarter,* **from** *January* **through** *March, was a real surprise.*

  Correct: *The flight* **between** *Cleveland* **and** *Toronto has been delayed.*

- To prevent confusion when linking open compounds or some terms that already contain hyphens

  Correct: *That music is from the post–World War I era.*

  Correct: *It was a combined high school–junior high event.*

  Correct: *A Labradoodle is a part-retriever–part-poodle hybrid.*

Note: You don't have to use an en dash every time you connect terms that contain hyphens. If the meaning is clear with hyphens alone, don't get fancy.

  Correct: *This translation is for our non-English-speaking friends.*

  Correct: *Chicken is a staple on fund-raising-friendly menus.*

- After a date, with nothing following, to indicate ongoing time

Correct: *John Smith (1953–) is the author.*

Correct: *The study (2002–) follows eight hundred subjects.*

> **Tip**
>
> En dashes should never have spaces around them, and em dashes can sit tight too. But some people prefer to give em dashes a little air. It's okay to add a space on both sides of an em dash — like this — but if you do, make sure you do it consistently.

Infinitives Can (and Sometimes Should) Come Apart

Back to some ghost-busting. You hereby have permission to go right ahead and split your infinitives (verbs with *to* in front of them) when the phrase demands it. Ms. Stickler meant well, but she was a slave to superstition. Keeping *to* and its verb together, come what may, has never been necessary in English grammar. It stifles the language, disregards idiom, and sometimes causes confusion. Let your ear—and the meaning—be your guide when fitting descriptors around verbs (*CMS* 5.106, 5.160; *Garner* 742–44; *WC* 98–100; *Woe* 182–83).

Sometimes a sentence sounds better when *to* and its verb stay together.

Natural phrasing: *We want you **to arrive** safely.*

Awkward phrasing: *We want you **to** safely **arrive**.*

But sometimes keeping an infinitive intact is a force fit.

Natural phrasing: *He decided **to** flatly **refuse** the offer.*

Awkward, ambiguous phrasing: *He decided **to refuse** the offer flatly.*

And sometimes it's impossible, without a complete overhaul.

Natural phrasing: *The storm is expected **to** more than **double** in strength.*

Drastic (and unnecessary) work-around: *The storm is expected **to be** more than twice as strong.*

Great writers of English have been splitting infinitives whenever the need arose for hundreds of years, and great editors have been letting them do it. Join the club.

T i p

The same thing is true for other multiword verbs. It's no more necessary to keep *soon* out of *will arrive* than it is to keep *summarily* out of *to dismiss*. You have enough to keep track of as an editor; don't add split-verb superstitions to your list.

Danglers Can Deceive

It starts innocently enough; then, trouble. *At four, Tina's birthday party was a huge success.* Who's four? Tina or Tina's party? The way this sentence reads, that party's been going on for years (maybe it *was* a huge success). Or maybe it was a success at four o'clock but a disaster at three-thirty.

When the start of a sentence describes something other than what comes next, the result can be confusing, even hilarious. To keep writing clear (and humor intentional), make sure the beginning of a sentence really applies to what follows and doesn't "dangle" (*CMS* 5.84; *Garner* 217–19; *WC* 291–94; *Woe* 159–66).

Correct: *Waving frantically, she got the cab to pick her up.*

Incorrect: *Waving frantically, the cab picked her up.* (The cab wasn't doing the waving.)

Numbers Need Consistency

Spelled out or numerals? Which one when? Without a little discipline, numbers can get unruly. Here are some guidelines to help you keep order. There are different ways to handle numbers, but what's important is to choose a system and apply it consistently (*CMS* 9.3–7, 9.10, 9.14, 9.19, 9.23, 9.59, 9.62, 15.71–72, 15.75).

System 1
- Spell out either one through nine or one through ninety-nine. (Pick one approach and stick to it.)
- In addition, spell out round numbers above ninety-nine (*three hundred*) and any number that starts a sentence.

System 2
- Spell out only single-digit numbers and numbers that start sentences.
- Use numerals for everything else.

With Either System
- Where many numbers appear together, if your chosen system requires a numeral for one item in a group of similar things, use numerals for all (*reports of 107 pages, 24 pages, and 5 pages*).
- However, to prevent confusion, you can mix styles (*six 4-story buildings, 12 six-story buildings*).
- Always use numerals with years, days of the month, and percentages (*2001, June 20, 6 percent*).
- When you use a numeral for money, use a symbol for the monetary unit; when you spell out the amount, spell out the monetary unit (*£12, eight cents, $3.95*).
- When a quantity is spelled out, spell out the unit of measure as well. Spell it out, too, if there's no common abbreviation for it (*five miles an hour, fifteen minutes, seven pounds, a 60-watt bulb*).
- When a unit of measure is abbreviated, or shown as a symbol, always use a numeral. Note that with the exception of time, abbreviations for units of measure are the same in the singular and the plural (*5 yd., 3 sq. mi., 34 m, 6″, 1 min., 8 yrs.*).
- Use an en dash (–), not a hyphen (-), in ranges of numbers (*2005–2006*).
- Except in page numbers, addresses, and four-digit years, use commas in numbers of 1,000 or more (*1,253; 10,000*). For very large numbers, use spelled-out words in addition to numerals (*2.3 million people, $5 billion*).

Punctuation Can Pile Up

Most of the time, it's no mystery where to put a period or any other piece of punctuation. But what do you do when different types of punctuation show up together? Which one has right of way? Here are a few simple rules to help you direct traffic.

With quotation marks (*CMS* 6.9; *Garner* 658–59; *Woe* 153–54):

- Periods and commas go *inside* quotation marks.

  Correct: *She used to tell me that there's "always room at the top."*

  Correct: *"There's always room at the top," she would say.*

- Colons and semicolons go *outside.*

  Correct: *Ben Franklin said, "Waste not, want not"; so did my mother.*

- Other punctuation goes *inside* if it's part of the quoted material, *outside* if it's not.

  Correct: *"For the first time, I really understand!" he told me.*

  Correct: *What exactly do you mean by "the right choice"?*

T i p

A note on quotes: Unless you're actually quoting someone, using a word in a special sense, or giving the title of a TV program, radio program, or part of a longer work, there's no need for quotation marks. If you use them for ordinary words, you might convey an ironic meaning you don't intend. Consider the difference between *The new feature is an upgrade* and *The new feature is an "upgrade"* (*CMS* 7.60; *Garner* 658; *Woe* 156).

With parentheses (*CMS* 6.103; *Garner* 658; *Woe* 143):

- Periods go *inside* parentheses if they enclose a separate and complete sentence.

  Correct: *Her vision inspired us all. (Optimism was her strong suit.)*

- Periods go *outside* if what's in the parentheses—even a complete sentence—is included in *another* sentence.

  Correct: *The information is in this handout (you'll find it on page 2).*

- Other punctuation is inside *only* if it's part of the parenthetical material.

  Correct: *Take your seat quickly (and quietly!); the play has just begun.*

> **Tip**
>
> Space bar update: These days, a single space is all that's needed between sentences and following any punctuation (including periods and colons). No more double-spacing. Really! (*CMS* 6.11)

Semicolons Are Sophisticated

We all wrote far too many sentences like this one in, ironically, grammar school:

The dog chased the cat up the tree, it was very frightened.

Leaving aside the problem of whether it was the cat or the tree that was scared (we'll assume the dog was feeling just fine, thank you), what else is wrong with the sentence?

Yes, you're right. It's not one complete sentence; it's two, separated by a comma. The dread *comma splice*, bane of Ms. Sticklers everywhere. Two complete thoughts not joined by *and, or,* or another conjunction. In this case, Ms. Stickler's red ink is justified. A comma used this way was, is, and probably always will be a serious faux pas.

There are two ways to salvage the situation. You can do the straightforward thing and actually make it two sentences.

The dog chased the cat up the tree. It was very frightened.

Or you can do the sophisticated thing and replace the comma with a semicolon.

The dog chased the cat up the tree; it was very frightened.

What's the difference? The two-sentence approach is a bit abrupt and choppy, but more important, if you want readers to understand that the second statement is in some way related to the first, you've left them to make that connection by themselves. The semicolon lets you highlight the relationship. Half period, half comma, it says, "What follows is another complete thought, but it's closely connected to this one."

Separating two complete but related thoughts not joined by a conjunction is the most common job for a semicolon, but there are others. Semicolons provide clarity (*CMS* 6.57–62; *Garner* 659–60; *Woe* 139):

- Before certain adverbs that come between complete thoughts—*accordingly, besides, hence, however, indeed, then, therefore,* and *thus*

  Correct: *I gave it to her yesterday; besides, she already knew about it.*

  Incorrect: *I gave it to her yesterday, besides, she already knew about it.*

- Between parts of a sentence that are especially long or complex, even if they're connected with a conjunction

  Correct: *He arrived suddenly with a mountain of luggage, a cockatoo, and a cat; but I was delighted to see him, and the animals, too.*

  Not quite as clear: *He arrived suddenly with a mountain of luggage, a cockatoo, and a cat, but I was delighted to see him, and the animals, too.*

- In a series with elements that have other punctuation

  Correct: *The designer chose blue, the color of the sky; green, the color of the trees; and yellow, the color of the sun.*

  Incorrect: *The designer chose blue, the color of the sky, green, the color of the trees, and yellow, the color of the sun.*

When used correctly, semicolons add clarity, a bit of subtlety, and a grown-up air to any writing. Now, about that terrified tree . . .

Colons Wear Coattails

These upright little fellows serve a pretty serious function, so you'd expect them to dress a bit differently. Commas can wear jeans, semicolons look fine in business casual, but colons need more proper attire. Their task is formal introductions. You'll see them most often (*CMS* 6.63–69; *Garner* 653–54; *Woe* 140–41):

- Before an explanation

  Correct: *I told him my requirements: perfect weather and two weeks off.*

- Before a list (either horizontal or vertical), especially with *as follows, the following*, and similar phrases

  Correct: *He wanted three things from the store: milk, eggs, and sardines.*

  Correct: *He wanted three things from the store, as follows:*
  - *Milk*
  - *Eggs*
  - *Sardines*

But there are places where a colon is just too much, like a tux at a barbecue. **Don't** use a colon:

- After *namely, for example,* or similar introductory terms (they're already doing the colon's job)

  Correct: *Our task was clear, namely, to find the leak and fix it.*

  Incorrect: *Our task was clear, namely: to find the leak and fix it.*

- When a series is introduced by a verb or a preposition

  Correct: *Her talk will **cover** planning, logistics, and funding.*

  Incorrect: *Her talk will **cover**: planning, logistics, and funding.*

Correct: *Henry showed up* **with** *tools, a truck, and a huge grin.*

Incorrect: *Henry showed up* **with***: tools, a truck, and a huge grin.*

Colons and Capitals. In text, should you capitalize the first word that follows a colon? It all depends. If what the colon introduces is *less* than a complete sentence (and doesn't start with a proper noun), then no.

Correct: *The house was three colors: teal, mauve, and gray.*

If what follows *is* a complete sentence, but just one, you can either cap the first word or not (but whichever way you choose, stick with it).

Correct: *Tom gave his opinion: he thought we should start fresh.*

Also correct: *Tom gave his opinion: He thought we should start fresh.*

If it's more than one sentence, then it's caps for all.

Correct: *The quandary was this: Should we go ahead without asking him? Or get his opinion but spoil the surprise?*

Which Word When?

Certain words cause more than their share of confusion. We've collared eight prominent pairs of these perps, lined them up, and given you what you need to straighten them out. For more miscreants, see "Words Most Often Confused," at the end of this chapter.

A or An?

In American English, use *a* if you pronounce the *h*, *an* if you don't. So it's *a hotel*, but *an hour*. And with an abbreviation, acronym, or number, the article you choose depends on how the short form is pronounced—*an * symbol, a URL, an 11-hour drive* (CMS 7.46; Garner 1; Woe 131).

Bad or Badly?

This choice trips nearly everyone. That's probably because you hear these two words used incorrectly so often that wrong starts sounding like right. But it's actually easy to keep them straight. Here's how:

The word you choose depends on whether you're describing *the condition of the subject* or *the action itself* (CMS 5.158; Garner 81; WC 101–2; Woe 92–93).

Adjectives describe nouns, and subjects are nouns (or pronouns). So if you want to describe the subject, you need an adjective. *Bad* is an adjective, in this case describing how the subject (*I*) feels.

Correct: *I feel **bad** that I forgot your birthday.*

Incorrect: *I feel **badly** that I forgot your birthday.*

Adverbs describe verbs (actions), not nouns. So if you want to describe how an action is performed, you need an adverb. *Badly* is an adverb, in this case describing the manner in which the subject (*he*) feels.

Correct: *With thick gloves on, he feels **badly**.*

Incorrect (for same meaning): *With thick gloves on, he feels **bad**.*

There. We hope you feel better.

It's or Its?

We don't know if anyone's keeping score, but if they were, we'd bet these are the most misused and confused little words in the language. We think that's understandable and that it's all the apostrophe's fault.

First you learn that apostrophes show ownership. Here it's just the opposite. *Now* you need to *omit* the apostrophe to show ownership. Because now you're dealing with a pronoun, not a noun. The book, desk, inkwell, what have you may be *Mother's*, *Fred's*, *the Grangers'*, *this family's*, or *the school's*, but when you replace all those nouns with pronouns, the thing becomes *hers*, *his*, *theirs*, *ours*, or *its*. No apostrophe in any of them. Ever.

And the apostrophe that appears in *its* almost-twin has nothing to do with possession. It's just a placeholder for what isn't there. *It's* is short for *it is* or *it has*. In this shortened form (a *contraction*), the apostrophe stands in for the missing *i* or *ha* (CMS 5.202; Garner 471; Woe 39–40). So, with that in mind:

Correct: *It's a wonder we made that deadline.*

Incorrect: *Its a wonder we made that deadline.*

Correct: *The tree shed **its** leaves.*

Incorrect: *The tree shed **it's** leaves.*

Correct: *The idea was **hers**.*

Incorrect: *The idea was **her's**.*

Got it? Good. Assert yourself over pesky apostrophes.

> **Tip**
>
> If you just can't remember the difference between two similar words, here's a trick to simplify your life: memorize how to use just *one* of them, then use the other in all other situations.

Less or Fewer?

Everything you need to know to make this choice you learned in kindergarten. Really. If you can count, you'll know which word to use where.

It's as simple as this: Use *less* if what's diminished doesn't come in countable units. Use *fewer* if it does (*CMS* 5.202; *Garner* 491–92; *WC* 193–94; *Woe* 100). For example:

Correct: *People eat **less** beef than they once did.*

Correct: *People eat **fewer** hamburgers than they once did.*

Correct: *This line is for five items or **fewer**.*

Incorrect: *This line is for five items or **less**.*

Like or As?

We consider ourselves fairly progressive sorts, but we're about to sound positively stuffy. We concede that in casual speech, *like* is steadily gaining ground as the word of choice when comparing two things. (It's also gaining ground as a meaningless noise and a stand-in for about half the verbs on the planet, but we won't, like, go there.)

In good writing, however, there's still a place for *as.* Join us on the barricades and help preserve a distinction that's worth making (*CMS* 5.173; *Garner* 496; *WC* 160–61; *Woe* 104).

To compare two things, use *like* before nouns that appear without verbs.

> **Correct:** *He entered the room **like a conquering hero.***

> **Incorrect (for same meaning):** *He entered the room **as a conquering hero.***

In the preceding example, changing *like* to *as* changes the meaning entirely. In the second sentence, he actually *is* a conquering hero, fresh from his achievement. In the first, he just struts around like one.

To compare two things when a verb is involved, use *as.*

> **Correct:** *She went there at noon, just **as he had done.***

> **Incorrect:** *She went there at noon, just **like he had done.***

Was or Were?

Is it *If I was* or *If I were?* *If* doesn't automatically make it *were.* The choice depends on the circumstances. If something really was or could have been the case, then *was* is correct. If you're discussing anything other than fact (like a suggestion, wish, or what-if), then it's *were* you want (*CMS* 5.114, 5.130; *Garner* 756; *Woe* 56–57).

> **Correct:** *If I **was** in charge that week, I don't remember it.*

> **Correct:** *If I **were** in charge, I'd make some changes.*

> **Incorrect:** *If I **was** in charge, I'd make some changes.*

Which or That?

The choice between *which* and *that* is the choice between information that's nice and information that's necessary. In American English, *that* introduces information (never set off by commas) necessary to the meaning of the sentence (*CMS* 5.60; *Garner* 782–83; *WC* 112–17; *Woe* 3–4).

Correct: *The report **that he filed yesterday** went unnoticed.* (But the one he filed the day before got lots of attention. The clause starting with *that* specifies one of several possible reports.)

Incorrect: *The report, **that he filed yesterday**, went unnoticed.*

Which introduces information (always set off by commas) that's supplementary and not necessary to the meaning of the sentence. You could leave the *which* section out and still get the right point across.

Correct: *The report, **which he filed yesterday**, went unnoticed.* (There's only one report, so no need to specify which one. The clause starting with *which* is just extra information.)

Incorrect: *The report **which he filed yesterday** went unnoticed.*

Note: Of course, *which* and *that* both have other uses, too; you don't need to break out the commas every time you see a *which* or banish them every time you see a *that*. Just stay on your toes when you see them at the start of clauses like these.

Who or *Whom*?

In casual speech, *whom* is used less and less these days. When was the last time someone asked you "Whom are you here to see?" But in writing, to be correct, *whom* still has its place. And that's not so difficult to locate.

Who and *whom* are pronouns, so you choose between them the same way you choose between *he* and *him*: subject or object? *Who* is a subject, so that means *who* does something. *Whom* is an object, so that means *whom* is the one it's done to or for, with, about, from, on, etc. (*CMS* 5.56; *Garner* 834–36; *WC* 136–38; *Woe* 6–10).

Correct: *You're the person **for whom** I brought it.*

Incorrect: *You're the person **who** I brought it for.*

Correct: *You're the person* **who** *I thought* **would do** *it.*

Incorrect: *You're the person* **whom** *I thought* **would do** *it.*

Correct: **Whom** *do you mean?*

Incorrect: **Who** *do you mean?*

Tools

Words Most Often Confused

The terms here perplex nearly everyone from time to time. Many sound similar but mean very different things. This list will help you keep them straight.

accept	to receive willingly
except	to exclude
advice	suggestion or counsel
advise	a verb meaning "to give advice"
affect	a verb meaning "to influence"
effect	a noun meaning "result"
all ready	prepared
already	previously
anxious	to anticipate with uneasiness
eager	to anticipate with enthusiasm
appraise	to place a value on something
apprise	to inform
awhile	an adverb ("he waited awhile")
a while	a noun ("he waited for a while")
biweekly	every two weeks
semiweekly	twice a week
bring	action toward you ("bring it to me")
take	action away from you ("take it to him")

capital	a seat of government (a city)
capitol	a building where a legislature meets
choose	to pick (in the present)
chose	picked (in the past)
cite	to quote
site	a location
compliment	praise
complement	something that completes or makes better
comprise	to include ("the whole comprises the parts")
compose	to be made of ("the parts compose the whole")
conscience	sense of morality
conscious	aware
convince	create or change a belief (use with *of*)
persuade	motivate to take an action (use with *to*)
e.g.	"for example"
i.e.	"that is"
ensure	to make certain
insure	to obtain insurance; to guarantee protection or safety
everyday	one word when used as an adjective
every day	each day
farther	at a greater distance
further	in addition to
faze	to disturb or disconcert
phase	a period or cycle
flair	a special talent
flare	a sudden bright light or an outward spread
flier	one who flies
flyer	an advertising circular
home (in)	zero in on a target
hone	sharpen

imply	to hint or suggest ("he implied it to me")
infer	to deduce ("I inferred his meaning")
later	afterward
latter	the second of two things
lay	to place or set down
lie	to recline
lets	allows
let's	contraction of *let us*
loose	not tight
lose	opposite of *win* or *find*
nauseous	causing nausea ("a nauseous smell")
nauseated	feel sick to one's stomach ("I'm nauseated")
passed	a verb; past tense of pass
past	a noun; the time before now
predominant	an adjective meaning "prevailing"
predominate	a verb meaning "to exert control over"
principal	main
principle	rule
stationary	not moving
stationery	paper
tack	a direction or approach ("a new tack")
tact	consideration for others' feelings
their	possessive of *they*
there	in that place
they're	contraction of *they are*
whose	shows ownership
who's	contraction of *who is* or *who has*

Words Most Often Misspelled

The following common words send people to the dictionary time and again. Save yourself the trip with a glance at this list.

accommodate	innuendo	receive
accumulate	inoculate	recommend
acknowledgment	judgment	restaurant
all right	liaison	rhythm
allotment	lightning	ridiculous
analyze	likelihood	separate
annihilate	liquefy	siege
benefit	maintenance	silhouette
bouillon	maneuver	skeptical
caffeine	necessary	sophomore
colonel	niece	spaghetti
conscientious	occasion	succeed
counterfeit	occurrence	supersede
discipline	parallel	surveillance
embarrass	paraphernalia	synonymous
entrepreneur	personnel	thorough
existence	pneumonia	tranquillity
familiar	precede	unanimous
fiery	prejudice	usage
fluorescent	privilege	vacuum
foreign	proceed	veterinarian
harass	process	waiver
height	questionnaire	weird
hemorrhage	realtor	withheld

Is It Correct? Checklist

There's a lot to keep track of as you seek editorial accuracy; more than you might imagine. The following checklist will remind you of what we've covered in this chapter, and a few bonus items, too. Keep it at hand as you work, to make sure you've looked for error everywhere.

Note: For a complete, three-part checklist that covers all aspects of editing, and for a professional-level eight-stage proofreading checklist, see Appendix B.

Is It Correct? Checklist	✔ First Reading	✔ Second Reading

Spelling and Capitalization

- Proper nouns, common words, and special terms are spelled and capitalized correctly. ☐ ☐
- Shortened forms (abbreviations and acronyms) are spelled and capitalized correctly and defined when first used or as needed. ☐ ☐
- Product names, trademarks, and registered trademarks are verified. ☐ ☐
- Titles, including the first and last word, are capitalized correctly. ☐ ☐
- Capitalization following colons in text is accurate:
    - Unless a proper name, lowercase when colon introduces less than a full sentence ☐ ☐
    - Consistently lowercase (unless a proper name) *or* capital letter when colon introduces a single sentence ☐ ☐
    - Capital letter when colon introduces two or more sentences ☐ ☐

Grammar

- Subjects and verbs agree (*I work, he works*). ☐ ☐
- Verbs are in correct tense (*I work, I worked, I had worked*, etc.). ☐ ☐
- Pronouns agree in gender and number with what (or whom) they refer to (*Tom and Bill rode **their** bikes; the tree dropped **its** leaves*). ☐ ☐
- Pronouns are correct according to their place in the sentence (*I gave it to **him**; he gave it to **me***). ☐ ☐
- Adjectives and adverbs are placed to keep meanings clear (*I drive on Friday **only** [other days, I walk]; I **only** drive on Friday [and do nothing else all day]*). ☐ ☐

Punctuation

General

- There is no missing punctuation. ☐ ☐
- There is no duplicated or misplaced punctuation. ☐ ☐

Apostrophes

- Apostrophes are used only for possessives (*Jane's*) and missing letters (*I'll; rock 'n' roll*), not for plurals (*two Janes; 1900s*). ☐ ☐
- Apostrophes face the correct way (*'04, not '04*). ☐ ☐

Commas

- A comma is used before the last item in a series (*Tom, Dick, and Harry*), unless chosen style omits it. ☐ ☐
- A comma, without a connecting conjunction, is not used to separate two complete sentences (use stronger punctuation, like a period or semicolon, instead). ☐ ☐

Dashes

- Em dashes (—) are used correctly—in pairs if they're in the middle of a sentence (consistently with spaces or not)—to set off words, and are the width of a capital *M*. ☐ ☐
- To replace the word *to* or *through*, an en dash (–) is used (with no spaces) to separate items in ranges (*London–Paris, 7 a.m.–9 a.m., 1999–2004*) and is half the width of an em dash. ☐ ☐

Hyphens

- Hyphenations and word divisions are correct (check a dictionary). ☐ ☐

Parentheses and Brackets

- There are always opening *and* closing parentheses and brackets. ☐ ☐

continued

Is It Correct? Checklist *(continued)*	✔ First Reading	✔ Second Reading
Periods		
• Period is *inside* parentheses when they enclose a separate and complete sentence.	☐	☐
• Period is *outside* parentheses when the parenthetical matter—even a complete sentence—is included in *another* sentence.	☐	☐
Quotation Marks		
• There are always opening *and* closing quotation marks as appropriate.	☐	☐
• Single quotation marks are used only around a quote within a quote.	☐	☐
• Periods and commas are inside quotation marks.	☐	☐
• Semicolons and colons are outside quotation marks.	☐	☐
• Other punctuation is inside or outside quotation marks, depending on whether it's part of the quoted item.	☐	☐
Lists		
• Numbered lists are used when sequence matters or items will be cited.	☐	☐
• Bulleted lists are used when sequence is unimportant and citation is unnecessary.	☐	☐
Figures, Graphs, and Art		
• Text references to figures, tables, and other elements are accurate and present as needed.	☐	☐
• Captions accurately describe graphics.	☐	☐
Sequence		
• Numbering in each numbered list is sequential and starts at 1 or A.	☐	☐
• Bulleted list items are in alphabetical order (unless another order makes more sense).	☐	☐
• Any section title numbering is consecutive.	☐	☐
• Heading levels (first, second, third, etc.) are styled correctly for the content they introduce.	☐	☐
• Numbered captions are in consecutive order.	☐	☐
• Page numbering is consecutive overall or within sections, as appropriate, and appears on all pages where it should.	☐	☐
Spacing		
• Words are separated by one (and only one) space.	☐	☐
• Periods and colons are followed by only one space.	☐	☐
Titles, Headers, and Footers		
• Titles and other headings accurately describe the content they introduce.	☐	☐
• Content of headers (at the top of the page) and footers (at the bottom) is correct for each section.	☐	☐
• Any numbering is consecutive and in appropriate form (e.g., all roman or all arabic).	☐	☐
• Spelling and capitalization are correct and consistent:		
-First letter after a colon is capitalized.	☐	☐
-First letter after an em dash or hyphen is capitalized or not, per style guidelines.	☐	☐
-Articles, short conjunctions, and short prepositions are lowercased, unless starting or ending a title, or contrary to style guidelines.	☐	☐
-First and last word are capitalized, regardless of part of speech.	☐	☐
Table of Contents		
• Entries exactly match headings that appear in the document.	☐	☐
• All headings appear that should (all first-level, all second-level, etc.); none appear that shouldn't.	☐	☐
• In electronic and Web documents, all links between table of contents and text sections work correctly.	☐	☐
Web Links		
• In electronic copy, Web links in text work correctly.	☐	☐

4

Is It Consistent?

Getting it right is one thing. *Keeping* it that way is another. It's all well and good to delete the hyphen from *best-seller* on page 3 (thank you, *Webster's*), but it's your job to make sure it's *best seller* in the six other places it appears, too.

And while it may not be your job to check facts with outside sources, it *is* your job to keep stated facts consistent with *each other*. If it's *General Smith* on page 10, it had better not be *Corporal Smith* on page 15 (unless he's been stripped of his stars or is having a flashback).

Catching errors consistently is the heart and soul of editorial review. And when it comes to consistency, the definition of *error* expands. Style choices, as much as any rule of grammar, determine what's "right." From the standpoint of spelling, grammar, or usage, it's no more correct to use *Figure* than *Fig.* to tag illustrations. But if *Fig.* is the style choice, *Figure* becomes a faux pas for the duration of the document.

We hear free spirits among you asking, "What's so important about consistency, anyway? What difference does it make if it's *Fig.* in one place and *Figure* in another?" In the case of General (Corporal?) Smith, the answer is easy: inconsistency equals confusion. And while readers might not be confused, exactly, by *Fig.* and *Figure*, some might pause to wonder—about the difference and about what other discrepancies might mar what they're reading. And that's not good.

Every item on every page, even a space, is there to tell the reader something, to aid in understanding. *This explains that. These things go together. This is a new idea.* If the same element is always used the same way to mean the same thing, readers will understand the message that much faster and better. If it isn't, readers can be distracted or confused, if only for a tiny, subliminal second. And that's all it takes to make them miss the point. There's a reason stop signs aren't red on one street and green on the next.

> **T i p**
>
> There's another good reason to insist on consistency: branding. In ads, market-
> ing materials, and other business communications, it's vital to their effectiveness
> and the company's image to keep logos, company names, product names, and
> so forth strictly uniform. If they are, people will never mistake one company or
> product for another, and they won't suspect the company of carelessness in more
> than its copy.

The number of things that can tend toward chaos in any piece of writing is surprising, really—far more than hyphens and commas and caps, oh my. There are conflicting facts, unruly indents, bullheaded bullets, frisky fonts, and lots more would-be mavericks. It takes a sharp eye and the right tools to rein them all in. We're here to help you with both.

Style Sheets, Revisited

Topping the list of consistency tools is the all-important style sheet you've made or received and faithfully updated (in case you haven't, see Chapter 2). For keeping things constant, there's simply no substitute for a style sheet. It's a memory aid that works on two levels.

First, you can check a term (or any other element) in the text against the one on the style sheet to be sure they match. If the one in the text is out of whack, you'll know what to do.

But how will you remember to check the style sheet in the first place? That's where the second level comes in. When you write something down on a style sheet, you'll remember *that* you wrote it, even if you don't remember exactly *what* you wrote. When you see the word, bullet, number, heading style, or whatever it is again in the text, a vigilant little corner of your mind will say, "Hey! That's something I need to verify." Even those of us who can't find our car keys have memories that work this way, and it's a good thing we do.

So your best ally in ensuring consistency will always be your style sheet. It's not just something else to keep track of; it helps *you* stay on track. Start it, tend it, keep it close, treat it like the friend it is. For a starter version and some sample entries, see Chapter 2, and for an advanced/professional version, see Appendix B.

Method, 1; Madness, 0

Along with your style sheet, you have another partner in the quest for consistency: a methodical, stepwise approach to your work. The stages of editorial review we described in Chapter 2 are almost as important as a style sheet in ensuring that nothing escapes notice. When you concentrate on just one thing, or a few similar things, at a time, you're far more likely to pick out the nonconformists.

A Crash Course in Consistency

You've got your style sheet and your stages; now, how do you sharpen your eyesight? Learning which areas might harbor rogue elements is a great way to start.

In the sections that follow, we'll alert you to items in writing that tend to need discipline. And at the end of the chapter, you'll find a checklist to help you keep track of them as you work.

Fast and Loose Facts

You've seen how easy it is to bust a general to a corporal. Talk about the power of words. People's names, titles, and ranks are always a place to look for discrepancies, but *any* fact can find itself contradicted.

The best way to keep content consistent is to stay a bit detached and keep questioning. "Does that make sense based on what she said earlier?" "Wait, wasn't it a *left*-handed lemur in the last section?" "How could he be in Houston and Helsinki at the same time?"

Spelling

Spelling might be the most obvious place to look for inconsistency, and it's not always all about typos. To be sure, a typo creates an inconsistency if the word is spelled correctly elsewhere. But what most typos really create is a simple misspelling. And one of those will usually leap out even if you're ~~sleeep~~sleep deprived.

Where Typos Can Hide. There *are* a couple of places where typos find cover. Blunders in type that's very large or in all caps can be all but invisible. For some reason, the bigger they are, the harder they are to see:

IT'S ESPECIALLY HARD TO SEE TYPOS IN ALL CAPS

Did you see it (*especialy*) quickly, or did you need another look? If you've spent any time reading headlines, you're already familiar with this pitfall.

It's also hard to spot a typo that results in a real word—the *wrong* word, but a real word nonetheless. Reading the familiar phrase *there's a change is the air*, you have to be wide awake to notice that *is* should be *in*. And no bits-and-bytes spell-checker will ever see it go by.

The only way to catch sneaky errors like these is to read word for word and character by character. When reading for pleasure or information, we all tend to read in phrases, leaving it to our minds to anticipate and fill in the words and letters our eyes might skip. Editors and proofreaders don't have that luxury. When doing editorial review, slow down and look, really *look*, at what's on the page.

Tip

If the spelling of any word causes you to hesitate, for even a second, reach for your dictionary. But you don't have to reach right then. Many people working on hard copy find it more convenient to tag questionable words, then go back and look them up all at once.

If you're using word processing software, you'll have a spell-checker waiting in the wings (or butting in at the hint of a typo, depending on your settings). Just keep in mind any spell-checker's blind spots and always trust yourself and your *Webster's* over anything that ends in .DIC.

How Do *You* Spell Democracy? Real spelling inconsistency appears when there's more than one correct way to spell a word and the author has used them both (or all). You'll see these changelings in *Webster's*, looking like this:

marshal *also* **marshall**

flügelhorn *or* **fluegelhorn**

For the sake of consistency, you need to pick one spelling per word and stick with it, but which valid option should you opt for? Many people think that when *Webster's* shows alternative spellings, the one listed first is the one it prefers. Not so.

This may come as a surprise, but *Webster's* never actually *prefers* anything. It simply reports how people are using the language (which is why, we kid you not, *hisself* is given space between *hiss* and *hissy*—what some of you might be having about now, but we digress). If there's any preferring to be done, it's done by the masses, not by experts in ivory towers.

When two or more possible spellings are shown for a word in *Webster's*, you need to know the code. The spelling you choose depends on two things:

1. Whether the word *also* or the word *or* appears between them

2. Whether or not they're shown alphabetically

If the word *also* comes between the two spellings, you can safely assume the first is the one most people use.

But if the word *or* comes between them, there's not much to steer by. If the two spellings are shown in alphabetical order, it's a coin toss. They're considered equally valid options, and neither is "preferred." Use whichever one you want (consistently) and have a nice day.

If the alternative spellings are *out* of alphabetical order, they're still considered equals, but the first spelling may be *slightly* more common than the second. There's more about what to infer when *also* and *or* both appear, but we won't drag you into it. It would just be cruel. (Look up *kitty-corner* if you're feeling masochistic.)

So in the preceding examples, if the author really uses one spelling about as much as the other, you should probably make it *marshal* and *flügelhorn* throughout, one because it appears first in its *also* entry, the other because it's out of alphabetical order in its *or* entry.

But if the author uses one valid spelling more than the other, by all means put that one on your style sheet and make it the norm. *Webster's* clearly won't care, and who knows? If you (and enough other people) use that spelling, it might appear first in the next edition.

The Long and the Short of It. Abbreviations and acronyms also love to act up. With these shortened forms, consistency can be compromised for a couple of reasons.

> **Tip**
> An abbreviation is a shortened form of a word (*Dr.*), an acronym is a term that's made from the first letters of a phrase and pronounced as a single word (*GUI*, pronounced "GOO ee," standing for *graphical user interface*), and an initialism is an acronym that's pronounced letter by letter (*SPCA*).

One reason short forms stray is the too-many-choices situation we just discussed. There are often at least two legitimate ways to abbreviate something, both familiar, so neither one simply *looks* wrong, the way *especialy* does. We've all seen both *Ala.* and *AL* standing in for Alabama, and unless a zip code is involved, either is correct. So it can take a keen eye (and maybe some caffeine) to catch an *AL* when the style sheet says *Ala.*

On the other hand, some short forms are so unfamiliar that a spelling deviation doesn't register as deviant. For instance (and with apologies to the International Society of Cardiovascular Surgeons), the acronym ISCVS is just so much alphabet soup to most of us. So if you were to see it ISVCS, you might not give it a second glance. At least not before you read this.

The first time you encounter an abbreviation or acronym, stop, verify both it and the correct spelling of the full term, and put them on your style sheet. Unless an abbreviation or acronym is well known to your audience, it's common to include the full, spelled-out version where the acronym first appears, then to use just the acronym thereafter. Every time you see that acronym, or any shortened form, slow down, read it carefully, double-check your style sheet, and verify that the full form has appeared as appropriate.

Tip

If the writing is rife with acronyms, make a separate list of them, either on paper or in an electronic file (the electronic version is always neater and easier to keep in alphabetical order). When an acronym is first spelled out in the text, add a check mark or something similar to it in the list. Then, later in the project, you can just glance at your list; you won't have to flip pages or run searches to know whether a short form has been defined.

Capitalization

Case is another hotbed of inconsistency. And that's hardly surprising. As you saw in Chapter 3, capitalization can be quirky, so people are often unsure of what's right when. Capital letters also confer importance, so some people and organizations have their own agendas when it comes to caps. Small wonder people waffle between *President* and *president.*

There are rules that govern uppercase letters (see "Capitals Can Clutter" in Chapter 3), but there are also choices to be made (by you or someone else) about what to capitalize—in job titles, in names of offices and institutions, in section titles, and so on. The sooner they're made and on your style sheet, the sooner you can start keeping capitals consistent. It won't take long for capital letters to start catching your attention.

Punctuation

In general text, two of the smallest punctuation marks are two of the most wayward: the hyphen and the comma.

Hyphens. These guys have plenty of rules to follow, but they have a hard time paying attention. They're the ones sitting in the back of the class, throwing spitballs at their cronies, the capital letters. Hyphens may be pint-sized delinquents, but you can restore order.

Take another look at "Hyphens Are Helpful (but Not Always Right)" in Chapter 3 and keep a good dictionary at your elbow to break up squabbles and settle end-of-line-word-break disputes. As you work, your style-sheet collection of hyphenated terms will grow, and you'll start catching inconsistent hyphens left and right, whether they're out of place or just plain absent.

Commas. Commas aren't quite as consistency challenged as hyphens. Grammar, not style, usually guides where commas go (see "Commas Are Crucial" in Chapter 3). But there are a couple of common comma situations that give you options, and you'll find yourself in at least one of them *all* the time. To maintain consistency in almost any document, you'll need to decide or confirm whether a comma will be used:

- **Before the last item in a series.** Will it be *red, white, and blue*, or *red, white and blue*? Depending on whether you're following *The Chicago Manual of Style* or *The Associated Press Stylebook*, either approach is technically correct, although for the sake of clarity we heartily endorse the former (called the *series*, or *serial* comma). Newspapers and magazines often choose to omit the last comma. But whichever convention you follow, follow it for every series.
- **Before and after *Inc., Jr., Sr., III*, etc.** Nowadays it's perfectly proper to omit the commas around these add-ons. It's also just fine to keep them.

Your call. But once it's made, use commas consistently in pairs or consistently not at all.

Numbers

Numbers are some of the most style-conscious creatures in writing. There are lots of choices to be made and followed concerning them in just about everything you'll edit.

The biggest decision is usually this: *spelled out or numerals?* For help making it, see "Numbers Need Consistency" in Chapter 3. Once you've settled on a system, note all its quirks on your style sheet and make sure every number in the document conforms.

Numbers are used most often to specify quantities: *15 apples, four oranges, $600*. But keep in mind that they're used for other things, too. You'll also need to keep number style consistent in things like:

- **Phone numbers**—e.g., *555-234-6978* or *555.234.6978* or *(555) 234-6978*
- **Dates**—e.g., *15 June 2002* or *June 15, 2002* or *6/15/2002*
- **Time**—e.g., *ten o'clock* or *10 a.m.* or *10 A.M.*

Numbers can be truly unruly. Notice when they step out of line.

Fonts

Garamond. Helvetica. Cochin. Papyrus. The selection of typefaces just a drop-down away is pretty seductive. Not to mention the added charms of roman, **bold**, *italic*, and that show-off, ***bold italic***. With so much razzle-dazzle at their fingertips, it's hard for some writers to exercise restraint; harder still for them to maintain consistency. That's where you come in.

Like everything else on the written page, fonts convey information. Sixteen-point bold roman might mean "section title"; twelve-point bold italic might mean "second-level subhead." Regular italic might mean "new term" or "notice this," and a font that's different from anything else might set off a table. In each case, the font style helps orient readers by telling them instantly what *kind* of thing they're looking at.

That's why it's vital for you to be clear on the role of each font in a document, note it on the style sheet, and make sure it's always used where and how it should be. Here are some important places to keep fonts consistent:

- **In headings,** to signal level
- **In lists,** to set off lead-ins
- **In tables,** for titles, column heads, stubs, and other special features
- **In text,** for emphasis or new information

Icons and Symbols

Like fonts, icons and symbols are signposts. They're little graphical attention grabbers that announce *this is a warning* or *this is a tip* or anything else that's a recurring feature.

It doesn't take long to train readers; they quickly learn what to expect when they see a particular icon. So watch symbols carefully; make sure the Warning icon isn't used where the Tip icon should be, or vice versa.

> **T i p**
>
> A great way to ensure consistency in these graphical elements is to give them your undivided attention during a single short editing pass at the end of your work (see "Do It in Stages" in Chapter 2).

Vertical Lists

A vertical list seems like a simple thing, so why are they so tough to keep consistent?

You'll find every rowdy element in vertical lists that you find in horizontal text, and then some. So just assume that everything we've talked about so far also applies to lists, and we'll move right along to new rebellions that arise when information gets stacked.

List Introductions. Before you even get to the list, it's decision time: will you use a colon at the end of the text that introduces a vertical list, or will you use other (or no) punctuation, depending on the syntax?

She starts each day with:	or	*She starts each day with*
Yoga		*Yoga*
Tea		*Tea*
Pizza		*Pizza*

Some people draw a distinction between introductions that are full sentences and those that are not; some people watch to see whether the intro ends with a verb or preposition (no colon for those folks). Other people are particular about whether the words *as follows* or *the following* appear.

But most people just use the colon in all cases—it's a great way to draw attention to what follows, and most readers expect to see it before a list. And if a reader even *thinks* about looking for a lost colon, you've got a distracted reader.

Bullets, Numbers, or? If there's a real sequence or hierarchy involved, or if later you want to be able to say "in item 2 . . . ," numbers are the right choice. If no list item takes precedence over another, and you'll have no need to point out a particular one, then use bullets. There are also plenty of lists (especially multi-column lists) that have neither.

When adding doodads to list items, do what makes sense for the list at hand. But do it consistently; use the same kind of bullets or numbers or nothing for the same kind of list, wherever it appears.

> **Tip**
> Unless another order makes more sense (like listing important things first), arrange bulleted list items alphabetically. There's enough chaos in the world; why add to it?

Bullet and Number Styles. If you've so much as peeked into electronic formatting options, you know how many bullet and number styles there are, waiting, practically begging to be used. Small bullets, big bullets, round bullets, square bullets, open bullets, bullets that look like bullfrogs. Anything is possible. Large roman numerals, small roman numerals, arabic numerals. Numbers followed by periods, numbers followed by parentheses, "numerals" that are actually letters (a, b, c . . .). Clearly, your choices (and your style sheet entries) don't end with bullet versus number, alpha order versus other.

Never mind; don't be intimidated. Note early on what bullet and number styles will be used in your project and where. Then stubbornly stick to them. Sometimes lists have sublists, so you might want a couple of different bullet and number styles, but rarely more. Repeat after us: Simple is good. Simple is good.

Tip

Beyond your own sanity, and that of the reader, there's another reason to keep bullet and number styles to a minimum. Some word processing software (*cough* Word *cough*) gets notoriously freakish when asked to keep track of too many bullet and number styles in any one document. Bullets disappear, odd things turn up in their place, and all kinds of mayhem erupts. You can spend hours trying to restore order. Do yourself a favor and keep it basic. (For more on the quirks—and real virtues—of Word, see Chapter 6.)

Indents and Spacing. If there's something odd about a list, and you can't quite put your finger on it, take a look at the empty places. The spaces around and within a list—above and below the whole list and between list items, and indents before and after bullets and numbers—should be uniform from list to list throughout any piece of writing. Freewheeling list formatting distracts from the business at hand.

Capitalization. There are a few different ways to approach this one, too. Many times each item in a list begins with a capital letter, whether it's one word or a whole sentence. That's usually a good way to go. But sometimes lowercase is a valid choice:

- In multiple-choice quiz answers
- In multicolumn lists
- If desired, when list items complete an introductory sentence

As with bullets and numbers, settle on a style for a given type of list and keep it consistent throughout.

List Item Lead-Ins. These are the bits of text that announce the subject of a list item. In addition to ensuring that the same font and capitalization style is used for all of them, make sure the punctuation that follows is the same too, at least within any given list, and preferably in all lists. Depending on the wording, periods are a popular choice:

List lead-ins. These bits of text announce . . .

Em dashes are another:

> **List lead-ins**—bits of text that announce . . .

Commas aren't uncommon:

> **List lead-ins,** those bits of text that announce . . .

Neither are colons:

> **List lead-ins:** Bits of text that announce . . .

And sometimes, when the lead-in is part of a continuing sentence, no punctuation is needed:

> **List lead-ins** are those bits of text that announce . . .

Any of these is just fine, but a mix of them isn't. Whatever you do, do it consistently.

List Item Endings. Here's the deal. Unless you're using sentence-style punctuation (more on that shortly), all the items in any one list should end with the same punctuation or lack thereof.

Complete sentences end with periods, so if *any* list item is (or contains) a complete sentence, it sets the style for the whole list. *All* items in that list end with periods, whether they're complete sentences or not:

> *The high winds damaged:*
> - *Trees in the area.*
> - *Cars, trucks, and mobile homes.*
> - *Some roofs on older houses. Houses built since 1995 sustained no damage.*

If *no* list item is a complete sentence, then *none* of them, including the last one, end with a period:

The high winds damaged:
- *Trees in the area*
- *Cars, trucks, and mobile homes*
- *Some roofs on older houses*

This second example is the cleanest, most economical way to lay out items that complete a sentence begun in the introduction. But if you like, you can punctuate such a list the way you'd punctuate a sentence—commas after list items (or semicolons if the items have punctuation of their own) and a period at the end.

Personally, we don't think sentence-style list punctuation has much to recommend it. It doesn't really clarify anything, and it might do just the opposite, by cluttering up the page. If you stick with periods in lists that contain complete sentences and no periods (or other ending punctuation) in lists without them, you won't go wrong.

Parallel Structure. It's a whole lot easier to keep elements like lead-ins and punctuation consistent if the items in a list all have the same style of wording, or *parallel structure*. It's a big help to the reader, too.

Here's a list *without* parallel structure:

Rob had three objectives:
- *To learn how to fly*
- *Finding a job with an airline*
- *Retire early*

That mishmash of grammar is guaranteed to give most readers vertigo. These three items all start with a different verb form—for you grammar hounds, an infinitive, a gerund, and what's either an infinitive stripped of its *to* or an imperative. But you don't have to know grammar to know this mix is a mess.

Now here's the same list, tweaked into parallel shape:

Rob had three objectives:
- *To learn how to fly*
- *To find a job with an airline*
- *To retire early*

Much easier to absorb, isn't it? When all three have the same form, the message isn't mired in the syntax.

> ### Tip
> Parallel structure is important in more than lists. Whenever one idea relates to another, the reader can compare them far faster if the grammar stays constant and only the concepts change. For more on effective writing, see Chapter 5.

Tables

Because tables are just another way to list information, they share guidelines and pitfalls with bulleted and numbered lists. But with tables, that's just for starters. Tables have all kinds of features simple lists do not, and where there's a feature, there's usually a style decision to be made and made consistent.

We won't try to cover them all; if you want to delve into stubs, spanner heads, and other table trivia, go to Chapter 13 of *The Chicago Manual of Style*. And take a lunch—you'll be there awhile.

If you'd like to stick closer to home, you can make most tables consistent most of the time by paying special attention to:

Table Titles. Unless the topic of a table is perfectly clear from context, and the piece is fairly casual, most tables need titles. And the table titles in any one document need to conform in a surprising variety of ways. Here are some things to review and keep constant:

- **Numbering.** Will the tables be numbered? If so, how? Just *1, 2, 3, 4, 5 . . .* or by chapter or section: *4.1, 4.2, 4.3, 4.4, 4.5 . . .* ?
- **Wording.** Do titles use noun forms (*Schools testing for math skills*) or relative clauses (*Schools that test for math skills*)?
- **Capitalization.** Sentence style (*Schools testing for math skills*) or headline style (*Schools Testing for Math Skills*)?
- **Placement.** Flush left, indented, or centered?

Abbreviations and Numbers. Table cells are aptly named; think *tiny, cramped, confined*. Because of limited space in table cells, things that might be spelled out in general text are often shortened in tables. If you're using *versus* in general text, you might make it *vs.* in tables. In general text, it might be *four*, but in a table, *4*. Note any table-specific conventions on your style sheet and keep them consistent in all the tables in the document.

Table Breaks. If a table travels to a second page, but its column headings don't, readers can lose track of what the different columns mean. To help keep readers oriented, it's common to repeat the headings at the top of every page where the table appears. It's also common to add *continued*, either wherever a table breaks or when the reader must turn a page to see more. And it's common for those niceties to be overlooked.

Determine the etiquette for the outsized tables in your document, then make sure each one displays the proper table manners. (For working with tables in Word, see Chapter 6.)

Table Styles. Automatic table styles in word processing programs can make you almost as giddy as bullet styles—all-grid, no-grid, minimal-grid, shaded headings, shaded columns, colored headings . . . you get the idea.

Having all those options is great for the graphically challenged (and we're charter members of *that* club), but without some discretion, not so great for consistent communication.

Different material lends itself to different table styles, so having choices is a good thing. And having a few different table styles in a single piece of writing is fine, provided there are a few different types of material that need to be tabular. But it's important to make sure that the same type of material is always presented in the same style of table—so readers know what kind of information a table contains and so they can easily compare information from table to table.

Table Placement. Will tables be flush left, indented, centered, full width? Tables can scatter themselves all over pages, creating visual chaos for the reader. Make sure each type of table in your document has a standard placement, and see that it hits its mark.

Document Titles and Headings
We touched on this earlier, but titles and headings are such vital stars to steer by that keeping them consistent really deserves more attention.

Titles and headings are what organize writing into sections, topics, and subtopics. And like titled types everywhere, they're not the least bit democratic; their whole purpose is to maintain a pecking order.

In the world of editing, titles name whole works and large parts of works, like parts, chapters, and sections. Headings name topics within those sections and establish a hierarchy, from the general to the specific.

First-level, or A heads, are main topics; second-level, or B heads, are subtopics that branch off main topics; third-level, or C heads, are subordinate to Bs. All this regimental behavior keeps everyone clear on what relates to what and how. And to tell a part title from a chapter title, or a B head from a C head, you look to see how it's styled.

To keep these signposts perfectly clear, look for the TSP Trio:

- Typeface
- Size
- Placement

For any given level of heading, all three should be consistent. If the style for B heads is twelve-point Tahoma bold, flush left, with six points of space before and after, then every single B head in your document should have those specs. No excuses, no exceptions.

Tip

Call on the TSP Trio to help you keep more than just titles and headings consistent. Keep it in mind as you review lists, tables, captions, labels, page numbers, headers, footers, and tables of contents.

Captions and Labels

Here's the difference between captions and labels: Captions appear *near* illustrations, usually below them. Labels appear *within* illustrations to point out specific features:

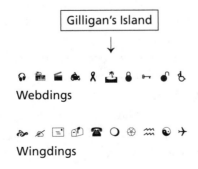

Fig. 5. Sample Webdings and Wingdings

Now that we've cleared that up, how do you keep them consistent? For captions, by first checking to see that their typeface, type size, and precise placement (TSP) are uniform. Then by making sure the following are all treated the same:

- **Numbering.** Captions don't necessarily require numbers, but if numbered is the style of choice in your document, then it's numbers for all. And if it is, are captions numbered in simple sequence or by chapter or section number first (like table titles)?
- **Abbreviations.** Remember the choice between *Figure* and *Fig.*? This is where to make it and follow it.
- **Wording.** Will captions be full sentences only, brief phrases, or a liberal mix?

Labels are more laid-back than captions. They usually work in pretty tight quarters, so wording is often just a word or two, abbreviations can be pretty brief, and placement is close to the thing labeled. Even so, watch for consistency in:

- **Font.** Label fonts are often smaller, lighter, or darker than other fonts.
- **Capitalization.** Lowercase, sentence-style capitalization, or headline style?
- **Connectors.** Are there arrows or fine lines that connect the labels and the labeled?
- **Background treatments.** Sometimes, where illustrations are dark, label text appears on an opaque white background and overlays the illustration; in light areas, label text might be placed directly on the illustration.

Page Numbers, Headers, and Footers

Headers and footers are the identifiers that run across the top and bottom of printed pages. Which is why they're also called "running heads" and "running feet." Too much pun potential there, so we'll stick to calling them headers and footers.

Headers in books traditionally contain information like book and/or chapter title and a page number (or in publishing parlance, a *folio*). Similar information appears in other types of documents, like press releases and newsletters. If it appears at the bottom of the page, it's called a *footer*.

If you're working with pages that are still in manuscript form, you probably won't have headers or footers to keep track of. But if you're working with formatted pages, either electronic or hard copy, it's likely you will.

As you work, do your best to be sure they contain the right information, styled and placed as and where they should be (think TSP) for each section of the document and for each left and right page. But don't expect to catch every glitch. Your attention early on will be more on the text than on the headers, and same ol'–same ol' headers or footers tend to look, well, the same after a while, even when they're *not*.

So at the end of your work, as one of your final passes, go back and look only at the headers and footers on each page, one by one. You'll probably be amazed at what you missed.

> **T i p**
> Watch out for a common header/footer error: frequently, numbering that should start over with each new section doesn't. If your project is numbered section by section, stay on your toes as the numbers flip by.

Tables of Contents

A table of contents may seem like a loner, but it's really a reflection. Every item in it matches one just like it, later in the document. Or *should*.

In manually compiled tables of contents, look out for:

- Wording variations between table of contents entries and text headings
- Missing entries
- Entries with no corresponding text heading

In automatically generated tables of contents, watch for:

- Missing entries (usually because text headings are misstyled)
- Entries at the wrong level (again, because text headings are misstyled)
- Too many entries (because too many heading levels have been picked up)

In all tables of contents, check oh-so-carefully to be sure all headings that should appear do and those that shouldn't appear don't. Make sure heading hierarchies are correct and the wording and spelling of all entries *exactly* matches the titles and headings that appear in the text.

Tools

Is It Consistent? Checklist
Consistency is all about detail, and nothing is better for keeping tabs on that than a checklist. Use this one to keep order in any document you review.

Note: For a complete, three-part checklist that covers all aspects of editing, and for a professional-level eight-stage proofreading checklist, see Appendix B.

Is It Consistent? Checklist	✔ First Reading	✔ Second Reading
Watch for consistency in . . .		
• Statements of fact	☐	☐
• Spelling (especially in acronyms and other all-capital items)	☐	☐
• Capitalization (especially in titles, abbreviations, acronyms, and following colons)	☐	☐
• Hyphenations and word divisions	☐	☐
• Last comma (or no last comma) in a series of items; commas or no commas around *Jr., Sr., Inc.,* etc.	☐	☐
• Numbers—either spelled out or numerals, and consistent style for area codes, phone numbers, dates, times, etc.	☐	☐
• Italic and other special fonts	☐	☐
• Icons and symbols	☐	☐
• Lists and tables:		
-Punctuation at the end of text that introduces the list or table	☐	☐
-Bullet and number styles	☐	☐
-Indents, spacing, and alignment	☐	☐
-Capital letters (or lowercase) at the start of each item	☐	☐
-Font, capitalization, and punctuation of list item lead-ins	☐	☐
-Punctuation at end of list items (either periods or no periods)	☐	☐
-Parallel structure	☐	☐
-Table title numbering (or not) and style	☐	☐
-Table-specific abbreviations (including numbers)	☐	☐
-Headings (and *continued* lines) for multipage tables	☐	☐
-Table placement and format styles	☐	☐
• Document titles and headings	☐	☐
• Captions and labels	☐	☐
• Page numbers, headers, and footers	☐	☐
• Table of contents entries	☐	☐

5

Is It Clear (and Compelling)?

If the writing is mechanically *correct* and internally *consistent*, you've already done much to make sure that it's *clear*. Add a sharp eye on undefined terms, words used contrary to *Webster's*, and the general sense of the discussion, and you've done what it takes to ensure clear, accurate communication.

But writing that's truly compelling is made of more. A piece that makes its point like an arrow and then lingers in the mind results from words used *well*, not just accurately. That's the goal of good authors—and one good editors help them achieve when asked to.

At less involved levels of editorial review, such as proofreading, fine phrasing and powerful prose are the author's job, not yours. At this level, ensuring accuracy and clear communication are all that's expected.

At more involved levels of editing, expectations can change. You may be asked to improve the writing by choosing a word, retooling a phrase, reshaping an introduction, or rewriting a whole section. Such things require editorial judgment, and judgment is subjective.

When your mission is to mold the writing, deciding what to change and what to let stand requires sensitivity to the language and the ability to think logically and independently. Those qualities can't be taught, but they can be honed. Most editors have them to some degree, or they wouldn't be editors in the first place. We expect you have them, too.

So in this chapter we'll help you fine-tune your editorial radar with some guidelines, pointers, and examples. We'll start by clarifying the scope of writing rehab you should attempt at each level of editorial review.

Proofreading

If you're doing standard proofreading (see definitions of levels of editorial review in Chapter 1), you're working hard to ensure clarity through correctness and consistency and by watching to be sure the discussion generally makes sense. If it doesn't, you query. But you're out of bounds to suggest more than minor wording changes.

You might point to a *which* that should be a *that* or note that *notorious* has been used three times in two sentences and suggest the author find an alternative. In standard proofreading, that's about all the writing reconstruction your job description covers.

If you're doing an editorial proofread, you're free—and expected—to do a bit more, but still nothing major. For example, at this editorial level, rather than simply suggesting the author find an alternative for *notorious*, you might actually go ahead and substitute the term *well-known*, particularly if you see that the intended meaning is "famous," not "infamous."

Copyediting

At the level of copyediting, you shape the language a bit more. Here you start to evaluate each sentence using different criteria: Is it wordy? Ambiguous? Repetitious? Appropriate for its audience? Logical? Does the main point stand out?

You also consider the work as a whole: Are the topics presented in an effective order, or would another order make the information clearer? Is the introduction engaging, the conclusion strong? Are there enough examples and illustrations—or maybe too many?

When you're copyediting, you ask yourself such questions constantly, but how many you ask and what you do with the answers depends on whether you've been asked to work with a light touch or a heavier one.

Light Copyediting

If you're doing a light copyedit, you correct obvious language errors and make relatively minor wording changes to clarify and tighten the message. You query terms that could confuse the reader. And you tend to any special issues you've been asked to address (e.g., rewording headings for consistency, eliminating contractions, changing passive constructions to active ones).

But you also let things go. You *don't* quibble with a bit of wordiness; you *don't* rework a slightly awkward sentence if its meaning is clear; you *don't* substitute a slightly better word for one that does the job.

If you run into areas that really need a rewrite, or major clarification, you simply query them and move on. That kind of heavy lifting isn't for light copyediting. Here's an example:

Original text: *In the ensuing period multimodal data transfer capabilities will be operationalized enterprisewide.*

Lightly copyedited text: *In the ensuing period, we will put multimodal data transfer capabilities into operation enterprisewide.*

> *{{Q: Will readers understand "multimodal data transfer capabilities"? If not, please define.}}*

Medium Copyediting

In a medium copyedit, you revise the language a bit more and query it a bit less. Here you have the green light to make more improvements, but you're still not rewriting whole sections wholesale or moving paragraphs around. Here's a medium copyedit:

Original text: *In the ensuing period multimodal data transfer capabilities will be operationalized enterprisewide.*

Moderately copyedited text: *Next quarter, we will begin multimodal data transfer throughout the company.*

> *{{Q: Is "next quarter" an accurate description of "the ensuing period"? Will readers understand "multimodal data transfer"? If not, please define.}}*

Heavy Copyediting

When an assignment calls for heavy copyediting, you're being asked to do more than brush up and smooth out the text. It's your job to decide whether the author's ideas have been presented in the best way and whether significant rewordings are in order. If they are, you can insert them. Here's the same bit of business-speak, heavily edited (into English):

Original text: *In the ensuing period multimodal data transfer capabilities will be operationalized enterprisewide.*

Heavily copyedited text: *Next quarter, we will begin to transfer data throughout the company in a variety of ways.*

Tip

Note that we said it's your job to clarify the *author's* ideas, because no matter how heavily you edit the writing, your objective is always to help the author communicate, to the best of your ability in a voice that's the author's. Under no circumstances should you simply replace the author's words with your words if the ones the author chose work just fine.

Substantive Editing

This is the most hands-on level of editing. It's also called *content editing*. It addresses not just *how* it's said but also *what's* said. Here you have license to simply rewrite chunks of text from scratch or reorganize the work to present the content more effectively, and if you think a different approach or different information would be helpful, you can ask the author to include it.

Most editors don't work at this level, but here's how our example might look if edited for substance:

Original text: *In the ensuing period multimodal data transfer capabilities will be operationalized enterprisewide.*

Substantively edited text: *Until now, we've had just one way to share data. Next quarter, we'll have a variety of new options.*

{{Q: Please detail the new options here.}}

It can be hard to draw lines between levels of editing; they're fluid, they blur, and it's a judgment call. But you'll need to make it, on a word-by-word basis, as you work. If you keep clearly in mind the level you've been asked to achieve, your decisions will be easier to make.

Where Clear and Compelling Come From

Let's assume you've been asked to pull out all the stops and make a piece of writing the best it can be. *This* piece of writing, for instance:

> *The first thing to point out is that there are many different types of reasons why writing needs editing. There's bad grammar, wrong words, confusing beginnings and that endings don't work. Some others are that it's hard to understand. Sometimes too things are repeated over and over, that's not necessary. Also, there are speling mistakes and punctuation. The list goes on and on, really. But editors ride in on their white horse and save the day. It gets all cleaned up and you and your business look good, even your prune-faced old English teacher wouldn't mind. Some people think editors are overpaid dinosaurs now that we have computers, but you'd be surprised.*

OK, it's hard to imagine you'd ever have to edit anything *that* bad. But work with us here. Let's take it apart and turn it into something clear and compelling (remember, you have carte blanche to dismantle and rewrite it).

The Level of Writing

First things first: is the level of writing suited to the audience? This piece is aimed at a general audience, not a specialized one. So from the standpoint of vocabulary, the writing level is about right. There are no highly technical terms, nothing the general public wouldn't understand.

The style, on the other hand, is more suited to an audience of middle-school students than an audience of adults. But we'll work on that.

The Overall Structure

Does the piece have a beginning, a middle, and an end? (Not really.) Is the sequence of topics logical and effective? (Somewhat; could stand improvement.) Do the paragraphs break at logical spots? (No; there's only one paragraph.) Do the sentences vary in length and structure? (Not much.) Are the transitions clear and graceful? (No.) Would some information work better in list form than paragraph form? (Yes.)

The Word Choice and Tone

Is the writing overly wordy, filled with clichés, ambiguous, or redundant? (In the extreme.) Are common words and expressions used appropriately? (Yes, for the most part.) Is the writing respectful and free of bias? (Not even close.) Does it contain strong images, active constructions, and parallel structure? (It's strong; we'll give it that.) Do pronouns have clear antecedents? (No.) Is humor used appropriately? (We're not sure we'd call it humor. Whatever it is isn't appropriate.)

The Clear and Compelling Makeover

With all those parameters in mind, let's rework the sample to make its points clear and its tone compelling to a general audience.

Here's the original, with commentary added to highlight the problem areas:

> *The first thing to point out is that there are many different types of reasons why writing needs editing.* [First sentence is very wordy, but the concept is a good place to start.] *There's bad grammar, wrong words, confusing beginnings and that endings don't work.* [Lack of subject-verb agreement, series comma missing before "and," and there's lack of parallel structure in "that endings don't work."] *Some others are that it's hard to understand.* [Lack of agreement between "Some others" and "it's," lack of a clear antecedent for "it"; this concept and others here would be better as brief list items.] *Sometimes too things are repeated over and over, that's not necessary.* [Missing commas around "too," redundancy, wordiness, and a comma splice.] *Also, there are speling mistakes and punctuation.* [There's at least one spelling mistake, and placement of *punctuation* makes it unclear whether punctuation errors or simply the presence of punctuation is the problem.] *The list goes on and on, really.* [Wordiness.] *But editors ride in on their white horse and save the day.* [Clichés, compounded by lack of agreement (are all editors on one horse?). A paragraph break would go well here, too.] *It gets all cleaned up and you and your business look good, even your prune-faced old English teacher wouldn't mind.* [Oh, yes she would. Starting with the murky "It," moving on to the ambiguity of "look good," another comma splice, the disrespect/inappropriate humor of "prune-faced old," and ending with the puzzlement of "wouldn't mind." Wouldn't mind what?] *Some people think editors are overpaid dinosaurs now that we have computers, but you'd be surprised.* ["Dinosaurs" is a cliché, and the reason that computers render editors antiquated needs explanation. So does exactly what you'd be surprised at and why. (We'll ignore "overpaid.")]

And here's one possible overhaul, with a global query at the end:

There are many different reasons why writing needs editing. Among them are:

- *Errors in grammar*
- *Errors in spelling and punctuation*
- *Errors in word choice*
- *Ineffective introductions and conclusions*
- *Confusing language*
- *Repetition*

Editors catch and correct these writing errors and many others. When they do, they protect the image and interests of authors and businesses alike. More than ever, in this age of constant communication, editors earn their keep. Computers provide tools like spell-checking, but there's still no substitute for human knowledge and judgment.

{{*Q: Have edits here preserved your meaning? If not, please alter as needed.*}}

Remember, this sort of clarification is done at only the most involved level of editing. If you're working with a lighter touch, you'll need to scale your changes accordingly.

For a convenient reminder of the clarity guidelines we've touched on here, for more tips on effective writing, and for unique clarity considerations when editing for specialized audiences, see the "Tools" section that follows.

Tools

12 Tips for Compelling Writing

Effective writing depends on two things—*what* you say and *how* you say it. These quick tips are especially useful if you're working in a business setting, but they'll help you shape writing of all kinds.

1. **Be brief.** Keep content—and titles—as short as possible to catch and hold readers' attention. Use bulleted lists instead of paragraphs where possible.

2. **Be specific.** For powerful, precise communication, get right to the point and say just what you mean. Instead of *Next we'll discuss sales. An*

improvement in sales was recently seen, write *We sold 12 percent more software last quarter.*

3. **Limit pronouns as sentence subjects.** Where possible, use nouns instead as the subjects of sentences. *It* and *they* can be ambiguous. *The dog chased the cat. It ran very fast.* Which is the speedy one?

4. **Use simple sentences.** Readers get lost in long sentences. To keep your message strong, try to limit each sentence to a single concept. Instead of connecting new thoughts with words like *however* and *whereas*, use a period and start a new sentence.

5. **Put important content first.** To catch your readers' attention, lead with your core conclusions; *then* show how you reached them.

6. **Stick to a single topic.** Try to discuss just one thing per article, memo, letter, or e-mail. Your point stands out when it stands alone.

7. **Know and target your audience.** Tailor your message to the knowledge and needs of your readers. Remember to define terms for those not familiar with them.

8. **Include a "call to action."** If you seek a specific result, spell it out. *The next time your phone rings, start keeping a phone log.*

9. **Address the reader with *you*.** Involve your readers by speaking to them directly. *When you plant a tree, you must water it.*

10. **Make it active, not passive.** Focus on who's doing it, not on what's done. Write *He called her*, not *She was called by him.* Unless the "doer" really doesn't matter, you'll save words and keep your readers awake.

11. **Be respectful.** Take care to avoid unintended insults and slights. Be alert to racial, ethnic, or gender bias in your words. *He or she* and *him or her* are here to stay. *They* and *their* (with a singular antecedent) are taking up residence, too.

12. **Use positives, not negatives.** Tell readers what they should do, not what they shouldn't do. Write *Please be prompt* instead of *Don't be late*. It's powerful psychology—one stresses the desired outcome, the other its opposite.

Wordiness Watch List

Wordiness and redundancy are the enemies of clear communication; editors work constantly to curtail them. Yet certain phrases are so common that we sometimes don't see them for the space fillers they are. The following list will alert you to some everyday excesses.

Wordy or Redundant Phrase	Suggested Alternative
advance planning	planning
assembled together	assembled
at some juncture	when
at this point in time	now
circle around back	regroup
cooperate together	cooperate
due to the fact that	because
enclosed herewith	enclosed
for the purpose of	to
fully cognizant of	know
in spite of the fact that	although
in the affirmative/negative	yes/no
in the field of	in
in the not too distant future	soon
in view of the fact that	because
join together	join
my personal choice	my choice
rarely ever	rarely
return back	return
small in size	small
the present incumbent	the incumbent

Buzzwords to Banish

Jargon is useful if it saves time and aids comprehension. People in technical settings use it as shorthand to communicate complex concepts. But in general speech and writing, particularly in business, jargon often loses real meaning. Certain catchphrases are used so much that the words become anything but catchy and often mean different things to different people. When that happens, jargon actually hinders precise communication. As you edit, stay alert to tired phrases and substitute standard English equivalents.

Buzzword/Catchphrase	Meaning/Alternative Wording
800-pound gorilla	largest or most important item, feature, person, etc.
actionable	can be readily done (*actionable* has a different, specific legal meaning)
Band-Aid	temporary fix
bandwidth	capacity
bring to the table	have to offer
bring *x* along	include, persuade
buy in (verb), buy-in (noun)	cooperate, cooperation; agree, agreement; consent
create energy around	promote
deliverable	a promised product or item
dialogue (verb)	talk with, speak to, discuss
dog and pony show	presentation
driver	agent of change
end-to-end	complete, comprehensive
enterprise	business, company
facilitate	help, make possible
from day one	from the start
functionality	functions, features
gain traction	gain influence or popularity
get a handle on	understand
going forward	in the future, from now on
granular	detailed
grow (a business, etc.)	enlarge, enhance, expand
hired gun	expert, consultant

incent, incentivize	encourage, influence
intellectual capital	knowledge
leverage	use an existing resource for another purpose
mission-critical	vital
net-net	final result
no-brainer	easy decision
offline	in private
on board	hired, committed to
on the same page	understand or talk about the same thing
paradigm shift	change in approach or thinking
push back (verb), pushback (noun)	resist, resistance
push the envelope	test the limits
ramp up/ramp down	increase/decrease
robust	reliable, works well
run it up the flagpole	test it for approval
scalable	flexible, expandable
solution	product or service
space	niche or market segment
step up to the plate	take responsibility
talking point	subject for discussion
turnkey	ready to operate
win-win	mutually beneficial
work-around	way to circumvent to a problem

Tip

Is it a technical term or just jargon? Here's how to decide: If there's a standard English word or brief phrase that means the same thing, you're probably dealing with jargon. If there's no ready synonym, you may need to use the special term.

Writing for the World: A Guide to Globalization

These days you don't need an office in Hong Kong or Bangalore to conduct business internationally. All you need is a Web site and a telephone, and the telephone is optional.

With a Web site, it's hard *not* to have a global presence. So it's increasingly important, as you edit, to keep in mind how American English will be understood by those who speak English as a second language and how it will translate to other languages and other cultures. These guidelines will alert you to things that might communicate clearly in Cleveland but cause confusion (or offend) in Amman or Seoul or Kiev.

- **Keep sentences short.** Long sentences are often grammatically complicated, so they're prone to mistranslation. To be sure the message remains clear, keep sentences simple.
- **Avoid words with multiple meanings.** For instance, instead of *it is hard*, write *it is difficult*. If you must use a term that's potentially confusing, put it in quotation marks when it's first used to indicate that it carries a special meaning: *Set it to control "widows" and "orphans."*
- **Include all articles and verbs.** To save time and space, people occasionally write in an abbreviated style—called *telegraphic*—that omits articles and verbs: *Managers to meet following presentation.* For a global audience, to avoid misunderstanding, flesh out the sentence completely: *The managers are to meet following the presentation.*
- **Keep *that*.** In English, especially in speech, we routinely drop the word *that* from our sentences. We often say "It is a process developed to improve quality," rather than "It is a process that was developed to improve quality." For nonnative speakers of English, the omission of *that* can cause confusion, so take care to use it, even though it makes for a longer sentence in English.
- **Limit acronyms.** Acronyms don't change in translation, so even if you spell out the words that form an acronym, those words, when translated, might start with different letters or appear in a different order, making the acronym itself confusing for someone who doesn't speak English.
- **Avoid humor.** What's funny in Chicago might be offensive in Kabul and fall flat in Nairobi. It's risky to presume you know what entertains those who live in another culture. When writing or editing for an international

audience, it's safest to use simple and respectful language and avoid humorous phrasing.

- **Watch for United States–centered wording.** When editing for a global audience, stay alert to the perspective—words like *foreign* and *non-U.S.* can appear ethnocentric and give offense. Similarly, be specific when referring to U.S. or state government agencies. Rather than *the federal government*, write *the U.S. federal government.* Other countries have federal governments, too.
- **Include state and country (if necessary) with city names.** An international audience will need to know whether you mean Cairo, Illinois, or Cairo, Egypt.
- **Specify time by date, not season.** Keep in mind that when it's springtime in Paris, it's fall in Sydney. Indicate time by date, month, or quarter, not by a season.
- **Avoid apostrophes.** Apostrophes aren't used in all languages, so some readers might not be familiar with them or what, in a contraction, they're intended to replace. To ensure clarity, spell out both words of a contraction. Use *it is* and *we will* instead of *it's* and *we'll*. For the same reason, avoid making words possessive by adding an apostrophe and an *s*. Instead of *the company's goals*, write *company goals* or *the goals of the company*.
- **Avoid exclamation points and ampersands.** Like apostrophes, these marks are not used in all written languages. To avoid puzzling some audiences, omit them in favor of other punctuation.
- **Avoid slashes.** A slash between two words can also be confusing. Instead of *and/or*, use simply *and* or *or*, or else write *either this or that or both*.
- **Be careful with graphics.** Symbols and icons that are widely understood in the United States may not be understood, or understood in the same way, in other countries. For instance, an octagonal red sign is not universally used to signal "stop"; use the word itself instead. Not everyone receives mail in a mailbox, and check marks don't communicate "verify" to people who don't use the word *check* in that sense.

Be especially sensitive to graphics that could be offensive or even obscene in certain cultures—particularly those showing interactions between the sexes, women in short skirts, hands (especially the left hand), and alcoholic beverages.

- **Avoid jargon and idioms.** By definition, jargon and idioms are words and phrases understood by a limited group. So naturally, when writing for a worldwide audience, it's vital to avoid such terms. Some idioms may seem like standard English, but if taken literally by a nonnative English speaker, they could be confusing. The following list offers examples of American-English idioms and suggests words and phrases to use instead.

Idiom to Avoid	Suggested Substitution
800 number	toll-free number
à la carte	individual
ad hoc	temporary, unplanned
as the saying goes	*The saying may not be known worldwide; rewrite to eliminate it.*
attack (as in *attack a problem*)	solve
besides	in addition to
bottom line	final result
bread and butter	primary revenue source
burnout	exhaustion
come up to speed	learn
connect the dots	put together, assemble
cutting edge	innovative, new
deal (noun)	transaction
deal with	manage
dozens	tens, many
draw on	rely on
drill down	analyze, research
drive	encourage, influence, lead, direct
explosion	increase, growth
flag (verb)	mark, highlight
free lunch	benefit, for free
from scratch, or the ground up	from the beginning
gear	equipment
geared toward	designed for, intended for
glue (verb)	bind
golden rule	primary principle
grow (as in a business)	enlarge, expand
handle (verb)	manage, process
hard to	difficult to
hassle	problem

hassle-free	trouble-free
holy grail	ultimate reward, ultimate goal
housekeeping	general administration
jump (in market movement)	increase
jump to conclusions	assume
keep an eye out	watch for
king	leader
left in the dust	outpaced
lion's share	majority
living hand to mouth	a marginal existence
look over	review
look to	desire to, choose to
make the grade	pass
master (noun)	leader, expert
nirvana	ultimate goal or reward
on the fly	in real time, hastily, spontaneously
on top of	in addition to
only game in town	sole opportunity
open the door to	lead to
out of the question	impossible
over	more than
pay off	be worth the effort
raise the bar	increase expectations
ready for prime time	prepared for
road warrior	mobile worker, salesperson
rule of thumb	general principle
short	brief
sliding scale	range
spam	junk e-mail, unsolicited e-mail
stick to	continue
streamline	simplify
sweet spot	niche, opportunity
tackle (a problem)	solve
think outside the box	think creatively
toe the line	adhere to the rule
turn the corner	achieve, reach
turnkey	complete, easily deployed
up and running	operating
with an eye toward	focus, goal

Is It Clear and Compelling? Checklist

Use the following checklist as you edit to help you ensure that any writing is as clear and compelling as it can be.

Note: For a complete, three-part checklist that covers all aspects of editing, and for a professional-level eight-part proofreading checklist, see Appendix B.

Is It Clear and Compelling? Checklist	✔ First Reading	✔ Second Reading
Sense, Flow, and Effectiveness		
• The level of writing is appropriate for the audience.	☐	☐
• The piece has an effective beginning, middle, and end.	☐	☐
• The sequence of topics is logical and effective.	☐	☐
• The language is not overly complex or wordy.	☐	☐
• The tone is respectful and free of bias.	☐	☐
• Wording is clear, and technical concepts and special terms are explained as appropriate.	☐	☐
• Conclusions flow logically from stated facts.	☐	☐
• Common words and expressions are used idiomatically.	☐	☐
• Pronouns have clear antecedents.	☐	☐
• Lists have parallel structure.	☐	☐
• Transitions are clear, graceful, and well placed.	☐	☐
• The writing contains strong images and active constructions.	☐	☐
• There is no ambiguity.	☐	☐
• There is no redundancy or repetition.	☐	☐
• Sentences vary in length and structure.	☐	☐
• There are neither too many nor too few paragraph breaks.	☐	☐
• Vertical lists or tables, rather than paragraphs, itemize information where appropriate.	☐	☐
• Examples and illustrations appear where needed.	☐	☐
• Any humor is appropriate and tasteful.	☐	☐

PART THREE

Onscreen and Online

More and more, writing, editing, and proofreading involve a keyboard and a screen rather than a pencil and sticky notes. And hallelujah, we say. Electronic editing is a boon beyond belief, provided you and the software are on speaking terms.

In this part we'll help you make three ubiquitous applications—Microsoft Word, Adobe Acrobat, and Microsoft PowerPoint—your editing friends. We'll also give you pointers for editing materials on and for the World Wide Web.

Where we could, we've been generic as we discuss electronic editing tools, but often we had to be specific. So keep in mind that the information in these chapters is based on the version and the default settings of the software noted.

If you're working with a different version, you may need to dig a bit to locate a particular tool or feature. And if your version is old enough, certain features might be missing. But for the most part, you should be able to find what you need with just a little hunting.

Also, we've made no attempt to tell you *every* way to do something; just the way or ways we've found useful. We're sure some of you will have found other, maybe easier, ways to use some of the features we discuss; congratulations, and could you send us an e-mail?

Electronic editing is here to stay and getting easier all the time. If you haven't dipped into the virtual pool, the chapters that follow will help you get wet. If you're in it already (maybe up to your neck), you might learn some new strokes.

6

Microsoft Word Documents

If you're an editor, Microsoft Word can be your best friend or your worst enemy.

It's your best friend because it is, no bones about it, *the* application of choice for editing an electronic file. In Word, changes are easy to mark, easy to see, and you'll never cramp your handwriting or wear down an eraser. You can add queries and comments all day long, with no rumpled sticky notes waving from the margins. You can find in seconds a single word (or a single character) in a thousand-page opus. You can finesse fonts and formatting with the flick of a mouse. And that's just for starters.

Some of us forget, and some of us never knew, how cumbersome editing was before Word laid its magic at our feet. And it's not just *easier* to edit using Word; with Word, you can actually *do better work*. When you compare the tools in Word to a red pencil and a stack of sticky notes, it's hard not to marvel.

But, hey, nothing's perfect. Anyone who uses Word knows it has a few quirks. If you're on a tight deadline, Word can seem like the enemy. It tends to *think* for you, and what it thinks might not be what you had in mind. It can also seem balky, obtuse, and downright capricious. Sometimes you want to yank back the curtain and have words with the little guy pulling the strings. We know. We've done our share of shouting at blameless computer screens.

But there is no little guy. Usually there's just a need to understand Word a bit better. There are one or two bona fide black holes in this application, but nearly always, if you know where Word keeps its tools and how to wield them, you can do remarkable things with minimal strain.

We assume that most of you have at least met Word. So we don't intend to tell you *everything* about it. You have the Word Help menu for that. Our goal is to help you make it a better friend. We'll show you Word's best editorial tools, reveal some of its shortcuts and secret passageways, and help you tap its huge potential.

All that will be easiest to follow if you have Word up and running as you read and if you have three toolbars open: Standard, Formatting, and Reviewing. So before you move on, go to View > Toolbars and make sure there's a check by each one.

Version alert: The discussion in this chapter is based on the default settings in Microsoft Word 2003.

Track Changes—the Better Red Pencil

To correct or improve writing, you have to make changes to it. If you're the author, working in Word, you can simply delete the old and type in the new. It's your work to craft as you please.

But if you're the editor or the proofreader, your changes are just *suggestions*, for the author or someone else to accept or reject. Those changes may be dazzling improvements, but they're nearly always still subject to review. It's the rare author or client who will trust you to tinker unattended. Most of the time, as you did in math class, you'll need to show your work.

On hard copy, you can't help showing your tracks. You mark changes by lining words out, writing words in, and using standard editorial marks (see Chapter 2). In the end, everyone can see what you've done.

In Word, to make your footprints visible (after you've saved the original file and created a working copy), you simply turn on Track Changes (Tools > Track Changes). Then you put your cursor where you want to add or delete text, start typing or start deleting, and the edits you make are colorfully apparent.

T i p

You can also toggle Track Changes on and off by clicking the Track Changes button on the Reviewing toolbar, by double-clicking TRK at the bottom of the screen, or by pressing Ctrl+Shift+E. (For more keyboard shortcuts, see the end of this chapter.)

It's hard to count all the ways Track Changes improves on a red pencil. We've already mentioned a few, and here are four more. With Track Changes:

1. No one needs to know editing symbols—you simply insert and delete text, and anyone can understand your changes. Even clients and authors who have never seen Track Changes can grasp the fundamentals in minutes—over the phone.

2. More than one editor can weigh in and do it clearly—it's easy to see who changed what, who asked what, who responded, and when.

3. It's easy for authors or reviewers to accept or reject your changes (more on that later).

4. Because no one needs to type in your changes (you've already done it), there's much less risk of *new* errors being introduced after the work leaves your hands.

Using Track Changes

You'll find all the Track Changes tools—your editing mainstays—on the Reviewing toolbar:

It contains, from left to right:

- **Display for Review** drop-down menu (ways to see your changes and the results of them)
- **Show** drop-down menu (which reviewing features to display and how)
- **Previous** button (moves you to the previous change)
- **Next** button (moves you to the next change)
- **Accept Change** button (accepts a change)
- **Reject Change/Delete Comment** button (rejects a change or deletes a comment)

- **Insert Comment** button (inserts a comment)
- **Highlight** drop-down menu (a rainbow of colors to highlight text)
- **Track Changes** button (activates and deactivates Track Changes)
- **Reviewing Pane** button (shows or hides the collected changes and comments)

Some of these need little explanation; others deserve some discussion. We'll start with what matters the most—how you show changes.

The Great Balloon Controversy. In the old days (before Word 2003), Track Changes lined through deletions and underlined insertions, using different colors for different editors. Formatting changes stood out in yet another color, and comments and queries showed up as highlights in the text, tagged with a number and the editor's initials. Here's how a bit of editing looked not so long ago:

People are complex~,~; their ~tolls~ tools should be simple.

That was then; this is now. These days Word edits have had an extreme makeover, moved to a place of their own, and remodeled it. Now they're in designer rectangles, off in the margin, which has been bumped out for their benefit. They have dashed and angled lines that tie them to their place in the text. Microsoft calls these rectangles *balloons*; some people enjoy them, and some people like the in-text markup better.

People are complex; their tools should be simple.
Deleted: .
Deleted: tolls

If you like the old-style edits, there's an easy way to pop these balloons and retreat to a simpler time. On the Reviewing toolbar, go to Show > Balloons > Never. It's a mantra that's made more than one editor's day. If you like your margins clean and clear, it might make yours, too.

> **Tip**
>
> If you choose *not* to use the balloons, be aware that you won't see formatting changes (such as roman changed to *italic* or **bold**) unless you visit your Track Changes options (Show > Options) and choose a way to make them visible. When balloons are set to Never, Word's default is to *make* formatting changes but not *mark* them.

If you're not an all-or-none person, you can straddle the fence; you can use old-style markup for insertions and deletions and balloons for comments and formatting changes (Show > Balloons > Only for Comments/Formatting).

> **Tip**
>
> If you're using balloons, you won't be able to zoom the page viewing size up very much. If you do, your balloons will start sailing off the right margin and you'll need to scroll horizontally to see them. Also be aware that even if you've embraced the balloons, you'll see them only in Print Layout View and Web Layout View. For more on these views, see the tip in the next section.

One Document Four Ways. For even more control over the way changes appear (or don't appear) onscreen, go to the Display for Review drop-down menu. There are four choices here, two with markup showing and two without.

While you're editing, you'll want to use Final Showing Markup. With Track Changes on, you'll see your insertions, deletions, comments, and—if you've chosen a way to make them visible under Show > Options—formatting changes. The first example is balloon free; the second is with balloons turned on:

Proofreaders pick up on the pickiest particulars[ME1].

Proofreaders pick up on the pickiest particulars

| Comment [ME1]: Deletion of second period okay? Have assumed this is not an ellipsis. |
| Deleted: . |
| Formatted: Font: Not Italic |

Some of the other options under Display for Review are good for special purposes. Final view shows you the document as it would look if all your changes had been accepted; no markup shows anywhere. This view is helpful to use as you do your final reading. Without all the markup, you'll see small errors—such as extra or missing spaces—more clearly and get a better sense of how well your changes really work.

Original view shows the text as it was before you made your first mark. It can be helpful to return to this view if you've made so many changes you've forgotten where you started.

If you're not using balloons, Original Showing Markup is almost identical to Final Showing Markup. The only difference is in how formatting changes are shown. If you *are* using balloons, the way insertions and deletions appear is reversed from the way they appear in Final Showing Markup. There must be a good use for this view, but to be honest, we haven't found one.

> **Tip**
> Besides the viewing choices you have on the Reviewing toolbar, you also have the five that appear under View or in the lower left corner of the screen—Normal, Web Layout, Print Layout, Outline, and Reading. To see all the art, comments, and other inserts in your document, be sure to view it in Print Layout View.

Having Your Say. There are two ways to add comments and queries in a Word document—using the built-in Comment feature and taking the do-it-yourself approach.

With Word's Comment Feature. To add a note using the Comment feature, place your cursor in the text where you want the note to appear and click Insert Comment on the Reviewing toolbar.

When you do, the word closest to your insertion will sport a pair of brackets and a highlight. If you're using balloons, one will appear in the margin, and you can type your note directly in it.

If you've banished balloons, a pane (the Reviewing Pane) will pop open at the bottom of the screen, giving you a spot to type your message. Type away, and when you're finished, close the pane by clicking the Reviewing Pane button on the toolbar.

If you're not using balloons, you'll see your initials (if the computer you're using is yours) and the number of the comment as part of the highlight in the text:

Editors are exacting; they're also [curious][ME2].

If you *are* using balloons, you'll see the comment number, your initials, and the text of the message all in the margin, in a shaded balloon. The highlight and brackets remain in the text, tied to the balloon by its dashed string:

Editors are exacting; they're also [curious],

Comment [ME2]: By curious, do you mean odd, or inquisitive?

Deleted: .

Whether or not you use balloons, when you insert a comment you'll always leave a highlight in the text. When the cursor is placed in the highlight, the text of the comment pops up, along with an incriminating little narrative of exactly who did what, when.

Merilee Eggleston, 10/20/2005 12:22:00 PM commented:
By curious, do you mean odd, or inquisitive?

Editors are exacting; they're also [curious][ME2].

There's no fudging your time sheet—this pop-up will tell the world your full name and *exactly* what day and time you inserted the comment. (The same thing applies to highlighted insertions and deletions. There's no place to hide.)

This electronic trail is a good thing, really; when more than one person is working on a file, it can be hard to tell at a glance whose changes are whose. But the pop-ups never lie.

T i p

If you want to make the text you're commenting on even easier to spot, you can highlight as much of it as you like *before* you click the Insert Comment button. That way, your Comment highlight will cover not just one word but a phrase, a sentence, or a whole section of text.

Directly in the Text. If you wish, you can bypass Word's Comment feature altogether and simply type your notes in the text. Some people prefer to see them that way. It's a great idea to bracket an in-text note with characters that aren't used (or aren't used in that combination) anywhere else in the document. That way the notes are easy to find by doing a search (see "Searching," later in the chapter) for that unique character or combination. You can also make such notes stand out with highlighting. For example (and imagine it in eye-popping pink):

{{Q: By curious, do you mean odd, or inquisitive?}}

> **Tip**
>
> Just because you *can* put queries of any length in a Word document doesn't mean you *should*. See Chapter 2 for a short course on query etiquette and strategy.

Reviewing. You may not be the only one adding comments or making changes to a Word file. Sometimes other people have chimed in before it ever gets to you. In that case, you'll probably want to look at their work before you do any of your own. And even if you *are* the only editor, at some point you'll want to review your changes one by one.

If you're using balloons, you can just run your eyes down the margin to spot and review each change or comment. If the changes are in the text only, step through them using the arrows on the Reviewing toolbar.

The Next (right-facing arrow) button pops you from one change or comment to the next, sequentially through the document. If you put your cursor at the top of the document and click the Next button, you can look at each change, one by one. If you want to go back for any reason, just click the Previous button.

> **Tip**
>
> Wherever there's a tracked change, Word puts a vertical line in the left margin next to it. If you're looking through a document for changes, without the help of Next and Previous, these thin rules will alert you to tiny things you might otherwise miss—a period here, a semicolon there, an extra space that doesn't belong.

Accept/Reject. Once changes and comments are made, someone must consider and act on them. That means accepting them, rejecting them, or adding something new.

There are times when you'll accept or reject changes made by others before continuing with your own work. You'll probably need to get an OK to do so. But usually the person who says yea or nay to changes is the author or whoever has requested the editorial work. If he or she isn't familiar with Word's Accept/Reject function, you'll be able to explain it in moments.

And those who are new to it almost invariably love it. Accept/Reject turns a marked-up manuscript into a finished file in very short order, and the process has an off-with-their-heads feel about it—click! this change stays; click! that one goes.

This imperial power resides in the check mark and the red X on the Reviewing toolbar. Place your cursor in a marked change or a balloon, then click the check mark to accept it or the X to reject it. If you accept it, the change becomes part of the finished document. If you reject it, it's gone before you can blink, and the text reverts to its original condition.

Word comments are never incorporated into the finished document (although the do-it-yourself, in-text variety can be because they're just inserted text; watch out, and see the warning that follows). Once a Word comment is dealt with, if it's a balloon you can reject it in the usual way. If you're not using balloons, just double-click the bracketed comment number area to highlight it, then click the Reject button or tap the Delete key.

Warning: Accept/Reject is incredibly quick and easy; sometimes *too* quick and *too* easy. In the drop-down menus next to the check mark and the X, you'll see several options for how *much* you accept or reject at a time. Unless you're absolutely positive that you know every last change in your document and want them all dealt with the same way, never, ever, choose an option that contains the word *All*. Take a little extra time and look at each change—or each group of changes (see the following Tip)—as you accept or reject it (or them). The global approach carries with it too much risk of losing or incorporating something you never meant to.

T i p

Even if the *All* options are too risky, you *can* safely accept or reject more than one change at a time. Just highlight a section that contains several changes, all of which you want to *either* accept or reject, then click the check mark or the X. It's a way to speed up the process and still keep an eye on what stays and what goes.

Beyond Track Changes

The Reviewing toolbar holds most of the electronic editing tools you'll need, but not all. Word's other menus and toolbars help you with more than markup.

Checking Spelling and Grammar

Word's spell-checker is something you'll use on every single item you edit in this application, once you're done with all your changes. Put the cursor at the top of your document and click the ABC check mark button in the Standard toolbar. The spell-checker will pick up some things you don't want it to, but for the most part you'll be glad you ran it. It's a lot of insurance against silly and embarrassing errors for a very small investment in time.

> **Tip**
>
> **Warning:** While Word's spell-checker is a boon, it also has some blind spots. Keep in mind that it will never squawk about a bona fide word, even if that word is the result of a typo. For instance, it will never let you know that you've typed *his* when you meant to type *this*, or *its* when it should have been *it's*.

Word's grammar checker, on the other hand, is a mixed blessing at best (OK, we hate it, and so does everybody else we know). This bit-bound curmudgeon is about as nuanced as a three-dollar calculator and as sensitive to the language as a visitor from Mars. Maybe less. It's simply wrong most of the time—or else catering to outdated grammar fetishes.

Sure, you can go to Tools > Spelling and Grammar > Options > Settings and uncheck most of its pet peeves, but at that point, why bother to use it at all? Save yourself the irritation and just go to Tools > Options > Spelling and Grammar and uncheck anything under Grammar. For *real* help with grammar, see Chapter 3.

Searching

Remember when we said you can actually *do better work* editing in Word? The Find feature (Edit > Find) is a big part of why. Another name for it might be the Consistency Checker.

As you work, you'll come across details that seem inconsistent—a spelling here, a heading style there, a capital letter someplace else—and you'll want to make sure that item is treated the same throughout. With a hard-copy document, ensuring such consistency depends on your memory, your eyesight, and how much time you have to comb through the work. In the end, you can only *hope* you've caught all anomalies.

But with Word's Find feature, you can search, in seconds, for the tiniest detail in the longest document. The items you collect on your search list (see Chapter 2) can be dispatched very quickly, and when you're done, you'll *know* you've seen them all.

To make things even easier and more consistent, you can use the Find and Replace option. Just type in what you're looking for and what you'd like to replace it with. You can make the substitution on a case-by-case basis, or with a single click of Replace All (but be as leery of this as you are of Accept All Changes).

Tip

Oops. You didn't mean to delete that word, you didn't mean to accept that change, you don't like what you just wrote, you were aiming for italic and not underline. For almost anything you do that you'd like to *undo*, there's the backward-swooping (Undo Typing) blue arrow on the Standard toolbar. Simpler still, there's the key combination Ctrl+Z. We can't imagine life without it.

Find is a powerful tool, and it lets you refine your searches in *very* useful ways. Click the More button on the Find tab to see the possibilities. Don't forget to click the Format and Special tabs, too. With these options and some creative thinking, Find will take you directly to almost anything in your document.

Tip

Find and Replace is one place where, sometimes, if you're careful, it just might be safe to choose the *All* option. For instance, if you know you want to change all hyphens in ranges of numbers to en dashes, you could use the Special menu under Find to set up a search for *Any Digit-Any Digit* and replace it with *Any Digit^=Any Digit* (the caret–equal sign combo is the code Find inserts when you choose "En Dash"). Then click Replace All, and it's done.

Inserting Breaks

In Word, comments are just one of the things you can insert. Authors often insert pictures, diagrams, hyperlinks, Excel files, and objects from other places. As the editor, you probably won't do that kind of inserting.

But if you're responsible for the final look and function of a document, you'll often insert *breaks*. Word has several different kinds (Insert > Break):

Page Break. This is the break you'll use most often. It simply ends one page and starts a new one—a useful way to split sections of text where *you* want to rather than where bottom margins dictate.

Column Break. In multicolumn text, you can insert a column break wherever you like, to control where material falls and to balance uneven columns.

Text Wrapping Break. This break forces text to wrap to a new line wherever you insert the break. You can accomplish the same thing by pressing Shift+Enter.

Section Break. A section break ends a section of text and starts a new one, so the formatting of the new section can be different from the one that just ended. There are four different kinds of section breaks:

- **Next page.** This is just like a page break, except that it starts a new section as well as a new page.
- **Continuous.** This doesn't force a new page; it just begins a new *part* of a page. For instance, Word inserts a continuous page break automatically when you highlight a section of text and format it as multiple columns.
- **Even page.** This break starts a new section on a new page, and that page will have an even number. So if you insert it on an even page, there will be a blank odd page between the two.
- **Odd page.** This is the same as an even page break, except that the new page *it* starts is an odd page. If you insert the break on an odd page, you'll get a blank even page between the two.

Inserting Symbols

The symbols on your keyboard barely scratch the surface of what you can include in a Word document. You have more dingbats, doodads, and doohickeys at your fingertips than you can imagine (or ever use). Just go to Insert > Symbol and take a peek under Font.

If it's a clever icon you want, try Webdings or Wingdings. If you need mathematical operators, something in Cyrillic, or a Greek diacritic, look under Subset. Whatever you need, it's there.

If you want to insert something more mundane—an em dash, for instance—go to the Special Characters tab.

> ### Tip
> If there are symbols you use often, it's easiest to insert them with a keystroke combination, or shortcut. Look on the Symbol dialog for an existing shortcut or make one of your own by clicking the Shortcut Key button.

Alphabetizing

Or, as Word would have it, Sorting. This is a great time-saver if you know where to find it.

To sort any list into alphabetical order, highlight it, go to Table (yes, Table) > Sort, and choose Paragraph and Ascending under Sort By. Then click OK, and provided your list items are on separate lines followed by paragraph returns, they'll be in alphabetical order.

A simple process, but not without quirks. For instance, if you have extra paragraph returns in your list, Word will remove all the extra spaces from the list and pile them at the start (so much for your manual formatting). It will also put numbers at the beginning, and it sorts *them* digit by digit, not quantity by quantity:

1
17
3

In addition, Word belongs to the word-by-word rather than letter-by-letter school of alphabetizing. So you'll see:

grand hotel
grand jury
granddaughter

Webster's would put *granddaughter* at the top. But these are small peccadilloes, not vexing enough to forgo the convenience of instant alphabetizing.

> ### Tip
> This function is a great way to keep your style sheet (see Chapter 2) in perfect alphabetical order no matter where you toss in new terms.

Formatting

Many times, production gurus, not editors, handle the finer points of formatting a Word document. But even if your focus is the words and not the window dressing, you'll need to format some items as a part of your editing.

And sometimes, particularly in business settings, whoever edits a document (report, newsletter, manual, etc.) also shines it up for printing and distribution. If that's your job, you'll need Word's formatting tools to do it.

And there are a lot of them. Word offers so many ways to alter the appearance of a document that we won't even pretend to cover them all. Instead we'll confine ourselves to the formatting tasks editors tackle most often and the things that sometimes make them grind their teeth.

Over the years we've spent way too much time fighting the formatting instead of tending the words, and we bet you have, too. Here are some ways to restore balance.

Make Word Less Helpful

Word wants so much to help. *Eager* just doesn't cover it. But you don't *always* want to replace a *c* in parentheses with a copyright symbol; you aren't *always* writing a letter when you type the word *Dear*. Sometimes you *do* want to type two capital letters in a row, and sometimes you *don't* want your quotes to curl. We know.

Here's how to curtail Word's default desire to please. Go to Tools > Auto-Correct options and uncheck everything you'd like Word to *stop* doing. Some items appear on more than one tab, so be sure to uncheck them wherever they appear. Then go to Tools > Options and do the same thing. If you're serious about controlling Word's impulses, pay special attention to the Compatibility tab you'll find there.

Take Advantage of the Toolbars

If formatting is part of your project, Word's Formatting toolbar will get almost as much of a workout as the Reviewing toolbar. With it you can:

Change the style, font, and point size of text:

Click on B for bold, I for italics, or U for underlining:

Left-align, center, right-align, and justify text:

Change the line spacing of text:

Create numbered or bulleted lists:

Choose a highlight color or a font color:

And in addition to the *real* basics, like opening, closing, saving, printing, cutting, copying, pasting, and spell-checking, the Basic toolbar contains editorial extras. On it you can:

Insert a table, choosing the number of rows and columns in it:

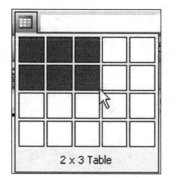

Create columns by highlighting text and choosing how many columns you'd like it to break into:

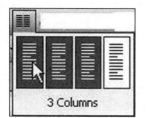

Show and hide formatting codes like paragraph marks, tab marks, and space marks:

View your document at a larger or smaller size (note that this is *viewing* it at a different size; changing the viewing percentage doesn't actually change the point size):

120%

You can choose a percentage from the drop-down list or type in your own percentage. Either way, be sure to return it to 100% and save that change if you're sending the file to someone else to review.

Make Yourself a Macro

To the technologically timid, this sounds daunting. And if you were going to actually *write* a macro, it probably would be. But Word lets you simply *record* one, and even gives you a toggle button (REC) to do it, right next to TRK at the bottom of the screen. It couldn't be less intimidating.

What *is* a macro? It's a little program that records a whole series of actions, then performs them, like a trick pony, whenever you tell it to. If you have the same formatting task(s) to do, over and over, macros can save you time and maybe even repetitive stress injuries.

For instance, let's say you need to change the first word of every list item in a three-hundred-page document from twelve-point Times New Roman to fourteen-point bold italic Tahoma. You can click in the first one, mouse up to the style drop-down, scroll down to and choose Tahoma, choose fourteen-point type, click on the bold button, and click on the italic button. Then you can do all that 179 more times.

Or you can click on the first word, double-click REC, name your macro, assign a keyboard shortcut to it or create a clickable toolbar button for it, whichever you prefer, and *then* go through all those other motions. When you've successfully changed the appearance of the word, stop recording your actions by double-clicking REC again or clicking Stop Recording on the little pop-up that appears while you're recording.

Now, for the remaining 179 font changes, all you have to do is place your cursor and tap a couple of keys or click a toolbar command. Which way sounds easier? Technophobes take note: macros save so much time (and wear and tear) that you can't afford *not* to record them.

Make Bullets and Numbers Behave

In our experience, nothing in Word is more likely to misbehave than bulleted and numbered lists. They may never reform entirely, but a few pointers should make them mind their manners (mostly):

Inserting Lists. Insert bulleted and numbered lists by clicking the Bullets and Numbering buttons on the Formatting toolbar or by going to Format > Bullets and Numbering. Don't insert them by manually adding spaces and typed-in numbers or inserted bullet images (from Insert > Symbol). If you do, you'll have alignment problems.

Setting List Indents. Control the indent distance from the margin, and the indent distance from the bullet or number to the start of the text, by setting tab stops on the horizontal ruler above your document or by specifying indents in the Customize Bulleted List dialog (go to Format > Bullets and Numbering, and click Customize). Set indents for an entire list by highlighting the whole list and then clicking tab stops on the horizontal ruler.

Tip

To indent all the text of a bulleted or numbered item, put your cursor in the paragraph and press Ctrl+T twice (if you have two tab stops set) to vertically align all text with the first letter following the bullet or number.

Managing Numbers. In long numbered lists, keep spacing consistent (and periods following numbers aligned) by choosing Right under "Number position" in the Customize Numbered List dialog.

To start list numbering over at 1, place your cursor in the first item of the list you want to renumber and choose "Restart numbering" on the Numbered tab of the Bullets and Numbering dialog. To continue list numbering from a previous list, choose "Continue previous list" on the same tab.

Managing Bullets. Choose bullet styles from those offered on the Bulleted tab of the Bullets and Numbering dialog or create your own in the Customize Bulleted List dialog. But be wary; if you use too many (more than two or three) bullet styles in a single document, strange things may happen. Bullets may suddenly disappear or be replaced by other things. No one, including Microsoft, seems to know why.

Tip

As you choose and use bullet and number styles, they'll be reflected in the choices you see when you open the Bullets and Numbering dialog. After a while, some of the original choices you saw there may be replaced by your more recent choices. To restore the default bullet and number style choices, just click the Reset button in that dialog.

Use Fonts with Finesse

The English alphabet may have twenty-six letters, but Word has about twenty-six thousand different ways you can display them. Font styles, sizes, and colors are available on the Formatting toolbar, but go to Format > Fonts to see *all* the possibilities. Choose small caps or all caps, strikethrough or underline, super-script or subscript, and other special treatments. For subtle adjustments, look to the Character Spacing tab; for gaudy options, go to the Text Effects tab.

Set the Spacing

The space bar and the Enter key have their place, but don't count on them for everything. You'll have much more flexibility, and your document will be much more orderly, if you use the spacing and alignment options on the Formatting toolbar or under Format > Paragraph.

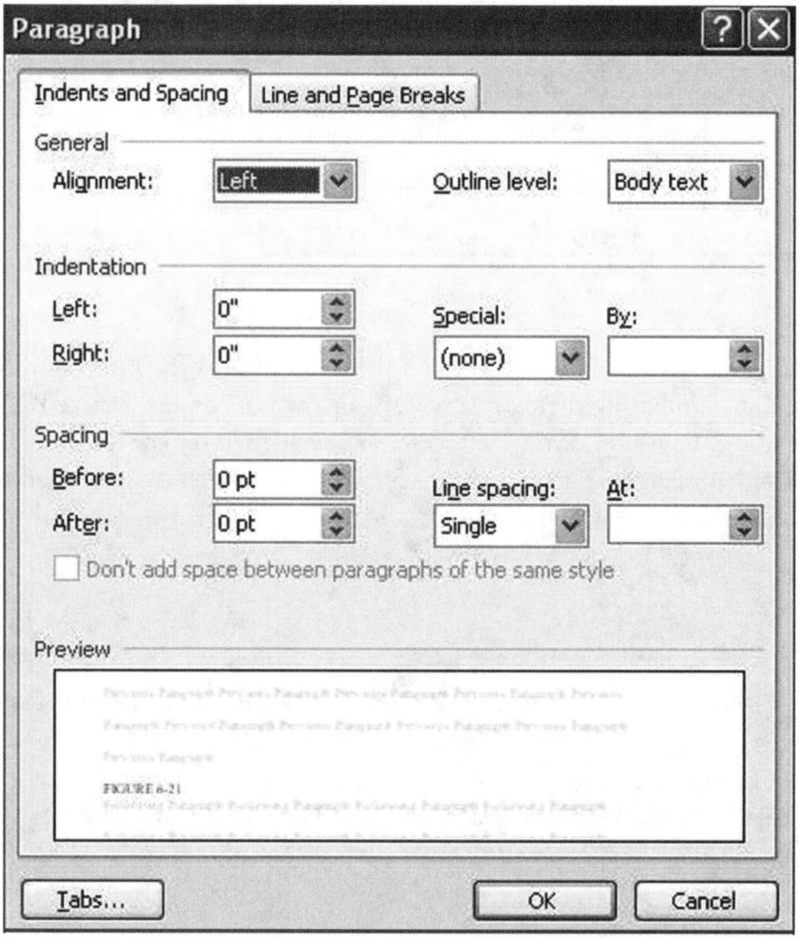

FIGURE 6-21

The two tabs in the Paragraph dialog let you control indents and alignment (left, right, center, or justified) of text, line spacing and the spacing before and after any element, and where pages and paragraphs break and don't break, among other things.

If you want to make sure a heading and the text that follows it don't appear on two different pages, you don't need to add extra hard returns to force the heading to the page where it belongs. Just put your cursor in the heading and check "Keep with next" on the Line and Page Breaks tab. That way, wherever the next paragraph goes, the heading will follow.

Tip

"Keep with next" really means just that. If your heading doesn't move when you select that option, it may be because what's next is a paragraph return between the heading and the text it introduces. Apply "Keep with next" to the intervening paragraph return *also*, and both of them will stick, as a unit, to the text that follows. Better still, replace the extra paragraph return with space you define (see below).

Two of the most useful features in the Paragraph dialog are the Before and After options under Spacing. With these you can define how much space appears before and/or after headings, paragraphs of text, items in lists, items in tables, and anything else that needs a little air. Just place your cursor in a paragraph, or highlight a whole section, and specify your space. For perfectly consistent formatting, choose the same amount of space around the same type of item throughout your document.

Tip

If you're trying to squeeze just a *little* more onto a page, and that page has a list or two, here's a trick: highlight the list(s) and reduce the space between list items by a point or two. The reduction won't be noticeable, but it might give you the extra space you need.

If you're defining text elements with template styles (e.g., Heading 1, Normal, Bulleted List, etc.), you can use the Paragraph dialog just once to define spacing as a part of those styles (for the document you're working on only), so you don't have to apply it repeatedly from the Paragraph dialog or the Formatting toolbar.

For instance, if you want your Normal text to be double-spaced instead of the default single-spaced, go to Format > Styles and Formatting and right-click on Normal in the list of styles. Choose Modify, click Format, choose Paragraph (look familiar?), and select Double under Line spacing. Click OK on your way out, and now everything that's Normal style in your document will be double-spaced. You can make spacing and alignment adjustments to any style (and many other adjustments, too), and save yourself trips to the Paragraph dialog.

Take Tables in Stride

Lots of writing includes tables, so there's no sidestepping them. And there's no need to. Word does its best to make inserting, styling, and editing tables convenient and automatic. And its best is pretty good. Here's a collection of tips to take the terror out of tables:

Tables Longer Than One Page. If your table runs to more than one page, you'll need to decide where you want the table to break. If you want to allow Word to break the table automatically at the end of the page, but you want to make sure the break doesn't come in the middle of a row, *uncheck* "Allow row to break across pages" under Table > Table Properties > Row. That way Word will break the table only after a whole row.

If you want to break the table yourself, at a spot of your choosing, place your cursor in the row *below* the one you'd like to end with and insert a page break (Insert > Break > Page break or Ctrl+Enter). The table (and the page) will end with the row above it, and the row where you placed your cursor will move to the next page.

Repeating Heading Rows. When your table is more than one page long, you'll probably want the table headings to repeat on new pages. To be sure they do, highlight your heading row or rows and go to Table > Heading Rows Repeat. Click to activate this option. Blissfully simple.

Splitting and Merging. If for some reason you want to split a table into more than one piece, but leave the pieces on the same page, go to Table > Split Table.

To merge table cells, so two or more cells become a single cell, just highlight the cells and go to Table > Merge Cells. This is an easy way to create space for titles that cover more than one column.

	January Through March		April
North	12	24	10
South	15	6	12
East	7	14	9
West	4	3	17

To do the opposite—to divvy up one cell into two or more cells—highlight the cell, go to Table > Split Cells, and choose the number of columns and rows you want to create.

Deleting and Moving. If you highlight the entire contents of a table and click Delete, you'll delete only the words *within* the table. To delete the table itself, make sure the table is highlighted and then press Shift + Delete or go to Table > Delete > Table.

To position an entire table (flush left, center, flush right, etc.), look for the small boxed-cross icon that appears at the upper left of the table (in Print Layout view) when you run your cursor over the table. Click the cross to highlight the table, then move it just as you'd move text.

Advanced Options

Word's toolbox may not be bottomless, but there's no denying it's deep. Beyond markup, beyond comments, and even beyond formatting, Word has more gadgets to make your editorial life easier. Here are a few things you might like to do with them.

Add Automatic Tables of Contents

You can do some impressive things with Word fields, but they're a subject for independent study (and extra credit). We have a supply of gold stars for anyone who wants to do it.

Most of the time there's just one field you need to use: TOC. When you insert a TOC field, you insert an automatic table of contents, and that's worth knowing how to do.

A table of contents field picks up headings in the text and plops them, with their page numbers, according to their outline level, into a table of contents that reflects *exactly* what's in the document. In the process it makes all the entries in the table of contents links, so you can just press Ctrl, click anywhere in the entry, and go straight to that spot in the document. If you change the wording of a heading in the text, or it wraps to another page, or you delete a heading or add a whole new one, the table of contents will reflect it (see "Updating the Entries," later in the chapter). But only if you've styled your headings correctly.

Styling Your Headings. For an automatic table of contents to pick up text headings, the headings must be styled using named template styles—Chapter Title, Heading 1, A Head, that sort of thing—that are different from the styles used in the rest of the document. If your whole document is styled Normal, Word won't be able to differentiate the headings from the text.

Once you've highlighted a heading, you can give it a text style from the Style drop-down menu on the Formatting toolbar or under Format > Styles and Formatting.

Normal ▾

▪ Bullet1	¶
▪ **Bullet1 + Bold**	
▪ Bullet1 + Left: 0", First line: 0", Box: (Single solid line...	
Centered	
First line: 0.5"	
# Heading 1	¶
## *Heading 2*	¶
### Heading 3	¶
<u>Hyperlink</u>	a
Italic	
Italic, Pattern: 15%	
Normal	¶

From that location (or using the Styles and Formatting button on the Formatting toolbar), you can right-click on a style name, choose Modify, and do just about anything you like with heading styles. You can alter them (make them any size, any font, centered, flush left, underlined, outlined in lights—it's up to you) and name them anything you want. You can call your level 1 headings Ralph if you like.

Tip

Warning: When you create new styles or modify existing styles, make sure the Automatically Update box is *unchecked*. If it's not, and you make a manual change (say, italics for emphasis) to an individual item that carries a template style (say, a bulleted list item), you'll automatically change the style of *every* item in the document that carries that style. Editors discover whole new vocabularies when things like that happen.

The Table of Contents Options dialog (Insert > Reference > Index and Tables > Table of Contents > Options) shows you all the named styles in your document's style template and lets you assign a hierarchy (1, 2, 3, and so on) to the ones you choose (Ralph, for instance).

Once that's done, the TOC field will pick up everything in the document that carries the styles you've specified and tuck it into the table of contents, according to its designated level.

You can probably see this pitfall coming: *your table of contents will be only as accurate as your style definitions.* Computers read your mind only when you don't want them to, so for this whole thing to work, you must be careful to style every heading correctly and to use those styles for nothing else in your document.

Inserting the Table of Contents. With your headings styled, place your cursor in the document where you'd like the table of contents to appear (usually at the very beginning) and go to Insert > Reference > Index and Tables.

Index and Tables ☒

| Index | Table of Contents | Table of Figures | Table of Authorities |

Print Preview

Heading 1............................. 1

Heading 2........................ 3

Heading 3 5

Web Preview

Heading 1

Heading 2

Heading 3

☑ Show page numbers

☑ Right align page numbers

Tab leader: [....... ▼]

☑ Use hyperlinks instead of page numbers

General

Formats: [From template ▼]   Show levels: [3 ▲▼]

[Show Outlining Toolbar]   [Options...]   [Modify...]

[OK]   [Cancel]

If you like the defaults on the dialog that appears, and your heading styles match the styles shown, just click OK. An automatic table of contents springs to life next to your cursor. If you want to tweak the table's appearance, click Modify before you insert it.

Tip

Tables of contents (and other fields) show up shaded in text, but it's not really shading and it won't print. It just appears in the file to indicate an inserted field.

Updating the Entries. When your table of contents goes in, it reflects what's in the document *at that moment*. But if anything changes in the document, you'll need to update the table of contents before you see the changes there (so it's not completely "automatic").

Fortunately, updating is simple. Just place your cursor anywhere in the table and right-click. Choose Update Field and then decide whether you want to update the entire table or just the page numbers. You'll almost always want to update the entire table, to catch any little thing that's changed since the last time you updated. You'll want to be especially sure to do it at the end of your work, along with that final spell-check. It takes mere seconds, and it's good insurance.

There's another way (naturally) to update the table of contents. You can click Update TOC on the Outlining toolbar. There are two versions of this toolbar: the fully loaded and the lite. If you go to View > Outline, you'll see the full-featured version. If you go to View > Toolbars > Outlining, or click Show Outlining Toolbar on the Index and Tables dialog, you'll see a much-reduced version. On either version, you'll see Update TOC. Click it and proceed.

This (these?) toolbar(s?) offer some other handy options, too. To add an entry to your table of contents, just place your cursor in the item you want to add and choose the appropriate level from the Outline Level drop-down. Then update the table of contents; whatever you've just redefined will appear there.

Be forewarned, though: when you pick a level, you'll assign that level to the *entire paragraph* where your cursor resides. You can't select specific text by highlighting it. So be sure any headings you want to include are on lines of their own.

To remove an entry, you can assign it a level that doesn't appear in the table of contents (Body Text, for instance). To make either operation even easier, you can change text levels with the arrows next to the drop-down.

And if you want to quickly review heading levels in your document, go to the Show Level drop-down on the expanded version of the Outlining toolbar. There you can look at any one level of heading or all of them (for more, see "Check Heading Levels," later in the chapter).

Insert Hyperlinks

In a Word document, you can create clickable links to:

- Other places in the same document, such as the top of the document or a section within it
- Other documents on your hard drive or on your company's network
- Any Internet address

To insert a link, place your cursor where you want the link to appear and go to Insert > Hyperlink (or press Ctrl+K) and type the text of your link in the "Text to display:" field. Depending on the type of link you're inserting, Word will then help you navigate to your destination and complete the process.

Check the Word Count

If you're an author writing an article, you might be working toward a specific word count. For you, length is what matters.

If you're an editor or proofreader, time is what matters. How long will it take to complete an editorial project? In both cases, word count is key. Although the concept of a "page" has become a tad abstract in the electronic age, the standard way to estimate how long it will take to edit or proofread a document is still calculated using pages per hour.

In the days of hard-copy manuscripts, a page was defined as an 8½- by 11-inch double-spaced sheet. In a Word file, a page is considered 250–300 words. For help in estimating your time (or the length of your article), go to Tools > Word Count for the detailed numbers on your document.

> **Tip**
> The word count doesn't include comments you've inserted with the Comment feature, because they won't be part of the finished file. (If you've typed them directly in the text, however, comments *will* affect the word count.)

And if you'd like to keep *very* close tabs on the word count, choose the Show Toolbar option. With the Word Count toolbar open, you can check the count as often as you like just by clicking Recount.

Word Count

Statistics:

Pages	18
Words	1,123
Characters (no spaces)	5,439
Characters (with spaces)	6,417
Paragraphs	218
Lines	395

☐ Include footnotes and endnotes

[Show Toolbar]   [Close]

Compare Text

If you've used the text comparison tools Word keeps under Window, you probably wonder how you ever lived without them. If you haven't used them before, prepare for a treat.

What editor or proofreader doesn't frequently need to compare something in one document (or part of a document) with something in another? None that we know. Word makes it delightfully simple to do so—without constant scrolling or minimizing and maximizing.

To compare two documents side by side, go to Window and choose "Compare Side by Side with. . . ." To split one document horizontally into two independent sections, choose Split and then click in the document. To see and work with several documents on your screen at the same time, choose Arrange All. (When you apply Split, the option in the Window menu becomes Remove Split. Choose that when you want your document back in one piece, or else just grab the horizontal bar with your mouse and slide the bar off the top or bottom of your page.)

Once you have your desired combination, you can choose New Window to preserve that view as a separate document, so you can flip back and forth between your combined view and any other documents more easily.

> **Tip**
>
> When working with two or more documents on the same screen, the one that appears on the top (or the left) is the one you're viewing when you go to Window to make your comparison choices.

Check Heading Levels

It's an editor's (and a proofreader's) job to verify that all headings are handled consistently, in both formatting and wording. For example, your document style might require level-1 headings to be in all caps, set on their own lines, and worded as commands, and level-2 headings to be in bold italic, run into the text, and worded as questions. If your document is styled with Word's template styles (Heading 1, Heading 2, etc.), there's an easy way to check them for consistency.

Go to View > Outline, and your document will switch to Outline View. More important, the Outline toolbar will appear.

On the Show Level drop-down menu, you can choose to view all the headings in your document or only the heading levels you choose. Using this tool, you can quickly review your headings—with no distractions—to be sure they are as they should be.

Returning Finished Files

When you finish editing electronic files, and it's time to send them into the ether, they might be a little *large*. (That goes for *all* electronic files, such as PDFs and PowerPoints, as well as Word files.) Large files can make upload times long and e-mail servers cranky. Some e-mail programs compress files automatically, but some don't. If you fear your file is a beast, or you have several files to send, run it (or them) through a compression utility like WinZip or ZipIt. Then attach the streamlined version to your message.

And as a last step, always open your attached file *from* your e-mail message just before you send it, to be sure you've really attached the right thing. It can save so much confusion (take it from people who *know*).

Tools

Editing in Word—a Quick Reference

Word has a dizzying array of options, but the ones you'll use most as you edit can be pared down to a relative few. Here's a brief guide to working with Word's primary editing tools:

- ✔ **To turn Track Changes on or off:** Click the Track Changes button on the Reviewing toolbar, double-click TRK at the bottom of the screen, or press Ctrl+Shift+E.
- ✔ **To set markup options:** On the Reviewing toolbar, go to Show > Options and choose colors and styles for different types of changes.
- ✔ **To turn balloons on or off:** On the Reviewing toolbar, go to Show > Balloons and choose Always if you want to use them for all your changes, Never if you don't want to use them, or Only for Comments/Formatting if that's your preference. You can also choose balloon settings under Show > Options.

✔ **To set how changes are viewed:** On the Reviewing toolbar, from the Display for Review drop-down, choose Final Showing Markup while you're working, to see changes as you make them, and Final when you do your final reading, to get a clean view of the finished product.

✔ **To insert new text:** With Track Changes on, place your cursor where you want the new text and start typing.

✔ **To delete text:** With Track Changes on, place your cursor at the start of the text you want to delete and hold down the Delete key.

✔ **To add a comment:** Place your cursor at the spot in the text where you want to insert a comment, then go to the Reviewing toolbar and click Insert Comment. If you're using balloons, one will appear, and you can type your remarks in it. If you're not using balloons, the Reviewing Pane will open; type your comment there. To close the Reviewing Pane, click the Reviewing Pane button on the Reviewing toolbar. (If you want to bypass Word's commenting tool and just type your remark directly in the text, it's a good idea to set it off with something like double braces or asterisks to make searching for comments easy.)

✔ **To remove a comment:** If you're using balloons, highlight the balloon that contains the comment you want to remove and click the Reject Change/Delete Comment button on the Reviewing toolbar. If you're not using balloons, highlight the comment number bracketed in the text and press Delete or click the Reject Change/Delete Comment button on the Reviewing toolbar. (Naturally, if you've typed a comment directly in the text, just use the Delete key.)

✔ **To accept or reject changes:** Step forward through marked changes by clicking the Next button on the Reviewing toolbar. Step backward through them by clicking the Previous button. To accept a change, make sure it's highlighted, then click the Accept Change button. To reject one, click the Reject Change/Delete Comment button. Be *very* leery of choosing an Accept All or Reject All option.

✔ **To search:** Use the Find function under the Edit menu. Narrow your search with the options under the More button. Go to the Replace tab to automatically replace text once it's found (but be *very* leery of choosing Replace All).

✔ **To work with a split screen or multiple documents:** Go to Window and choose Split to create two independent halves of a single document; choose Arrange All to see and work with multiple documents on the screen at the same time; and choose "Compare Side by Side with . . ." to see and work with two documents side by side.

✔ **To spell-check your document:** Place the cursor at the beginning of the document and click the Spelling and Grammar button on the Basic toolbar.

Handy Keyboard Shortcuts

The Word menu options include some keyboard shortcuts, and the Help menu has many more. For your convenience, here's a list of some keys that can save you time and mousing. (**Note:** If you're working on a laptop, or a keyboard with a nonstandard configuration, in a few cases you might need to use different keys.)

Center a paragraph	Ctrl+E
Close	Ctrl+W
Copy	Ctrl+C
Create new document	Ctrl+N
Cut	Ctrl+X
Find	Ctrl+F
Go to	Ctrl+G
Help	F1 key
Insert a comment	Alt+Ctrl+M
Insert em dash	Alt+Ctrl+minus sign (not hyphen)
Insert en dash	Ctrl+minus sign (not hyphen)
Justify a paragraph	Ctrl+J
Left-align a paragraph	Ctrl+L
Open	Ctrl+O
Paste	Ctrl+V
Print Preview	Ctrl+F2 key
Print	Ctrl+P
Repeat an action	Ctrl+Y
Replace	Ctrl+H
Right-align a paragraph	Ctrl+R
Save As	F12 key

Save	Ctrl+S
Spelling and Grammar	F7 key
Split (screen)	Ctrl+Alt+S
Thesaurus	Shift+F7 key
Turn Track Changes on and off	Ctrl+Shift+E
Undo an action	Ctrl+Z

7

PDF Documents

Most electronic files are easy to alter. That's the good news and the bad. Good if you're writing or editing one, bad if you want to safeguard your original content. For instance, if you send a Word or Excel file into the world on its own, unprotected, almost anyone can rework it, intentionally or otherwise. If you're a lawyer or an accountant, the mere thought makes you cringe. So more and more, especially in business and professional settings, writers and designers are preserving their exact words, formatting, and art by saving files as Adobe Acrobat Portable Document Format (PDF) files.

A file saved as a PDF will appear exactly as its creator intended it to, regardless of who reads it or what platform displays it (Windows XP, Macintosh OS 10, etc.). And except in very limited ways and under very specific circumstances, no one else can directly alter that file without special permissions, such as for filling in blanks in a form. Any substantial changes to the material must be made in the application used to create the work in the first place, not in Adobe Acrobat.

For that reason, editorial review of a PDF poses special challenges. You can't just pull up the file and start inserting and deleting text, the way you would in a Word file. But your hands aren't entirely tied. Acrobat may be a great guardian of content, but it *does* allow you to express your editorial self. There are tools—some more convenient than others—that let you ask questions, suggest changes, and insert editorial marks.

Like a fat Swiss Army knife, Acrobat has a few tools that are indispensable and a lot more you *might* use sometime. In this chapter we won't cover every screwdriver and bottle opener, but we will show you all our editorial standbys—and a few other handy gadgets.

Version alert: The information in this chapter—especially about individual tools—is based on Adobe Acrobat Version 7.0 Standard. To mark changes in a PDF file, you'll need full Adobe Acrobat; with Acrobat Reader you can view a file and print it (and fill in some form fields), but nothing more.

Tip

When you have full Acrobat, it's supremely simple to create a PDF file. In most word processing, presentation, and spreadsheet applications, you have only to click the button or choose the option that lets you save your file as a PDF, then give that file a new name. You now have a PDF.

And if you want to restrict who can print or even open your document, go to Documents > Security > Show Security Settings for This Document. Choose the Security tab. You'll see a drop-down menu titled Security Method. The default is No Security, but choose Password Security and you'll find several ways to keep trespassers out.

Different Routes, Same Destination

Whether you're reviewing a Word file or a PDF, your job is still the same—to ensure that the content is correct, consistent, and clear. Here is a PDF file, as it appears in Acrobat 7.0, with some strategically inserted errors we'll ferret out later (thank you to Sandra and Cesar Estrada for the use—and abuse—of their Web page):

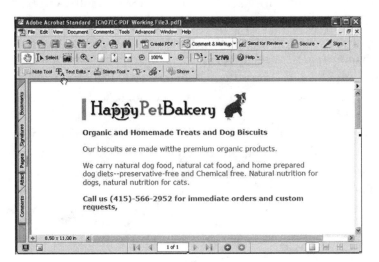

When you receive a PDF file for editing, you should treat it as you would any other electronic file—save it to your hard drive, preserving a clean copy of the original. Then use Save As to create your working copy, renaming it to indicate that it's an edited version.

At that point, you have several options. You can:

- Print out the file, mark your changes on the hard copy using standard editing marks, and fax back the changes
- Add your changes, suggestions, and queries to the electronic file, using one of Acrobat's built-in tools, and return the edited file electronically
- Do a combination of the two

Each of these approaches has its merits, depending on the situation. Let's look at them.

Working on Paper

There are several reasons to mark changes on a hard-copy printout of a PDF:

- **You prefer to mark changes on hard copy.** Some people feel they simply do a better job of catching errors when reviewing a hard copy.
- **The person who will receive your work prefers to see them that way.** Some people on the receiving end are more comfortable with hard copy, too.
- **You've been asked to fax the changes to whoever has requested the work.** Some people prefer you to fax changes to them, and that requires a marked-up hard copy, because in most cases fax transmission requires a paper original. Also, if you know you'll be faxing changes, you can take steps on a hard-copy document to make sure they are especially legible.

Marking Changes on Hard Copy. If you're working on hard copy, be sure to number the pages manually if page numbers don't already appear. You'll often return your corrections by fax, so mark changes very clearly, using standard editorial marks (see Chapter 2). Place any queries directly on the page, not too close to the edge. In fax transmission, material on page edges is sometimes lost or illegible.

If there isn't room to write everything clearly on the printout, create a separate sheet for changes and queries and simply note on the hard copy of the PDF page where the insertion or change belongs. On the separate changes/queries sheet, clearly indicate the location on the page where each change goes. One way to do that is to number the changes and place corresponding numbers on the PDF page printout.

Working on Paper and *Onscreen*

Sometimes you might want to *review* the contents of a PDF on hard copy but *mark changes* to it electronically. That's not as odd as it sounds. This split approach can be useful if your changes need to appear in the electronic file but:

- **You feel you're better at catching errors on hard copy.** As noted, some people think they are. If that's you, don't fight it. Work in the way that makes you most comfortable.
- **The PDF is exceptionally large or complex.** If it is, it may be more efficient to view all the text on a page at once instead of zooming in and zooming out, or zooming in, then constantly scrolling up, down, right, and left because the whole page won't fit on your screen.
- **You need to compare the text of a PDF to another document.** This could be a previous version in Word, for example, or another PDF. Or you may be reviewing, say, three documents that are very similar and you want to make sure the wording, graphics, and other details match in all of them.

> **Tip**
>
> If you plan to mark changes on hard copy and then transfer them to the electronic file, be *very* sure you don't miss a single squiggle. Account systematically for every change as you copy it. For example, put a check mark next to each change on the hard copy as you record it in the electronic file, and keep the hard copy until you're sure there will be no questions about what's on it.

Sometimes you might want to do the opposite. You might want to *review* the PDF in its electronic format but *mark changes* on hard copy.

For instance, if you've been asked to return your changes by fax, and you're working on a file that includes small type, it might be easier to read it onscreen so you can use Acrobat's indispensable Zoom feature (Tools > Zoom) to see these small things better.

> ### T i p
>
> Here's another trick to make tiny type easier to read:
>
> 1. Choose the Snapshot tool (more on using this tool later) to select one portion of text. This will copy text to the Clipboard.
>
> 2. Then go to Print. "Selected graphic" should be chosen under Print Range. Under Print Sealing, choose Print to Paper or a similar choice, depending on your print driver.
>
> 3. Click OK, and now when you print, the selected text is enlarged to fill the entire page. Much easier to read (for you and the person you're returning the changes to).

If you're reviewing onscreen and zooming in and out a lot, be careful not to skip any text that needs to be reviewed. In advertising brochures, for example, there might be three separate "spreads" (layouts) of text and graphics, all appearing on one PDF page.

If you need to zoom in to increase the size of small text, you may be seeing only one portion or one spread. When you return the file to the normal size, it's easy to lose track of where you left off reading. For situations like this, print out the file and use it in conjunction with the electronic version.

If you're reading the electronic file, you can also use the Find feature to quickly locate things that would be needles in a hard-copy haystack. When you come across a page that contains an error, you can print that page out and mark the change, then fax back only the pages that require revision (see "Print with Comments Summary," later in the chapter).

> ### T i p
>
> If for some reason you need to fax your changes or e-mail them separately from the PDF file you might find it convenient to record the changes on an electronic reporting form like the one discussed in Chapter 9 under "Using an Electronic Reporting Form."

Working Onscreen Only

If you're indicating your changes in the electronic file, you'll quickly find that Acrobat shares some things with Word, but not others:

- Many of the main menu options are the same in the two applications. If you're familiar with Word (or anything else made by Microsoft), you'll see a lot of old friends on the menu bar. You'll also see some strangers.
- In Word, you can insert and delete text and graphics to your heart's content, using Track Changes to show what you've done. Acrobat contains nothing similar to Track Changes, and you can't simply add or delete text; in most cases you must suggest changes by inserting a comment, near but not in the text.
- In Word, you can check spelling and grammar in both comments and text with the click of a button. In Acrobat, you can do it in one place but not the other (more on that under "Check Spelling," toward the end of the chapter).

Acrobat does contain Text Edits tools, and as enticing as that sounds, you probably won't use them much, if at all. Acrobat also offers what it terms Advanced Editing tools, including the TouchUp Text tool, which under some circumstances allows you to make limited editorial changes directly to the PDF, but for the most part these tools address page-formatting issues such as cropping, not writing issues such as commas or small wording changes.

Instead, for practical reasons, edits to text are almost always made as *comments*, and you can insert most of them using just a couple of Acrobat's Commenting tools—Highlight Text, and Note.

T i p

The easiest way to activate any Acrobat tool is to click it on its toolbar. We recommend you keep, at minimum, the following toolbars open while you work: Basic, Commenting, File, Tasks, and Zoom. To select them, go to View > Toolbars.

The Tools You'll Use (or See) the Most

We'll talk about prime editing options in a minute, but first, time out for *the Hand*. If you're new to PDFs, we know you're asking "What's the little hand thingy, and how do I make it go away?" (Admit it, you are. We did.)

The Hand Tool

The hand thingy (aka the Hand tool) wandering around your screen is, for some reason, Acrobat's default tool. It does what the scroll bars do—moves your document up, down, left, and right—but in a slightly creepy, disembodied, Cousin Itt sort of way. When you click the Hand tool, hold down the left mouse button, and move your mouse, the little white fingers clutch the page and pull it. You almost expect the paper to wrinkle. We're all for intuitive interfaces, but this one always makes us flinch a bit. Never mind.

The important part: how to make it go away. If you want Cousin Itt to scuttle back into his box, you'll have to select another tool. Or you may just have to get used to him.

Tip

Some Acrobat tools, such as the Hand, stay selected until you activate another tool. You can't toggle them off by clicking them a second time, the way you can a Word tool.

Some tools, such as the Note tool, *don't* automatically stay selected. You must activate them each time you want to use them. For instance, if you're using the Note tool, once you've written and closed your note, the cursor immediately reverts to a Hand. The next time you want to insert a note, even if it's two words later, you must select the Note tool again from the Comments or Tools menus or click the Note tool icon on the toolbar. If you're inserting lots of notes, that can get a bit old.

Here's help: You can keep any tool turned on until you activate a different one by selecting that tool and going to View > Toolbars > Properties Bar. Then choose Keep Tool Selected. Now, until you select another one, you can use the tool repeatedly with no mouse visits to a menu or toolbar.

The Top-Drawer Editorial Tools

In a PDF, you can efficiently do most of your editing using just two tools—the Highlight Text tool (our hands-down favorite) and the Note tool. The Pencil tool is good for a few things, too. Each of these tools gives you a different way to insert instructions, ask questions, and suggest changes, depending on what's most convenient for you or most appropriate for the work at hand.

Look for them all under Comments or under Tools on the main menu bar. Here's where the Highlight Text and Note tools are in the winding river of options under Comments:

The Highlight Text Tool. We've already declared our devotion to this tool, and soon you'll see why. If you want to master just one PDF editing tool, make it this one. Here's how:

1. Click on the Highlight Text tool in the Commenting toolbar or go to Comments > Commenting Tools > Highlighting > Highlight Text Tool and select it.

2. Using your cursor, highlight the text your comments will refer to.

3. Click in the highlighted area. An empty pop-up box will appear, ready for your message.

tural dog food, nat | **Highlight**   11/12/2005 5:33:49 PM ☒
preservative-free an | kd   Options ▶
ral nutrition for cats.
                     | Change to two words, no hyphen:
15)-566-2952 for
                     | preservative free

T i p

If you'd like the highlighted text itself to appear in the box, preceding your comments, go to Comments > Commenting Preferences, and under Making Comments, check "Copy selected text into Highlight," "Cross-Out," and "Underline comment pop-ups."

Using the preceding example, you would highlight the text in question and then double-click. If you've set your preferences as described, when the pop-up opens, it will say *preservative-free* (the original text). Below that, you would type in your comment: *Change to two words, no hyphen: preservative free.*

---

tural dog food, na | **Highlight**   11/12/2005 5:33:49 PM ☒
preservative-free a | kd   Options ▶
ral nutrition for cat | preservative-free
15)-566-2952 for
                    | Change to two words, no hyphen:

                    | preservative free

4. When you finish entering your comments, close the pop-up box by clicking the X in the corner. The highlighting will remain, along with a very small Note icon right next to it. The text of your note becomes visible when anyone passes a cursor over the highlighting or double-clicks in it.

Tip

Whether your changes appear when a cursor passes over the highlighting or when the Note icon is double-clicked depends on the version of Acrobat you're using. To be safe, suggest to those who will read your notes that they may need to double-click on the Note icon.

(Huge) Advantages: The Highlight Text tool, unlike the Note tool, lets you add a comment while obscuring little if any text. Also, your note always stays connected to the highlighted text; the same can't be said for the Note tool. And it's nice to be able to show the pertinent word or term in the text box.

Disadvantage: With this tool, some people worry that, because the highlight is within the text, a note inserted this way might be missed by the reviewer. We think that's unlikely, particularly because each highlight also travels with a little icon.

Tip

The default color for notes and highlights in Acrobat is yellow. If yellow sets your teeth on edge, and you want all your insertions to appear in, say, tranquil turquoise, right-click on a comment that appears in the offending color, choose Properties, and select your favorite color. Then, to make your new choice the default color, right-click on the comment and choose Make Current Properties Default.

If you want to use different colors for different comments, right-click on an individual comment, choose Properties, and select the color of your choice for that comment.

The Note Tool. Think of this as an electronic sticky note. It gives you a place—at any spot in the text—to jot whatever you wish. Compared to the Highlight Text tool, it has a few drawbacks, but it has its virtues, too. To use it:

1. Click on the Note tool in the Commenting toolbar or go to Comments > Commenting Tools > Note Tool and select it.

2. Place your cursor in the file where you'd like your note to appear.

3. Click. A Note icon will appear, along with a semitransparent box where you can type your message—request a change, ask a question, whatever you need to do.

food,
Chemical fr

| Note | 11/12/2005 5:38:47 PM ⊠ |
| kd | Options ▶ |

Lowercase "chemical"

ımediate c

4. When you're done typing your message, close the box by clicking the small X in the corner. The Note icon will remain visible, and your message will appear when someone runs a cursor over it or double-clicks on the icon.

food
Chemical f

Advantages: The default is a bright yellow note, so your message is easy to spot. It also gives you a way to insert comments in places where you can't use the Highlight Text tool (like multicolumn text).

Disadvantage: The Note icon itself obscures the text beneath it, so to see all the text, the reviewer may need to drag the icon (and the note along with it) to another spot. At that point it may be hard to tell what the note refers to.

Tip

To edit any comment you've made, open it with a double-click and make your changes. If you want to delete one you've written, click on it once. It will turn black. Then just tap the Delete key on your keyboard . . . and it's gone. If you've inserted a note but haven't yet typed in any text, you can remove it with the Undo function—Ctrl+Z.

The Pencil Tool. This is a Drawing tool, like the Arrow, Rectangle, Oval, and other Drawing tools. In general, the Drawing tools are used to create PDFs, not edit them, but the Pencil tool is the exception. With it (and enough dexterity) you can make standard editing marks on a PDF file just as you would with a real pencil on a printed page. To use it:

1. Click the Pencil tool in the Drawing toolbar or go to Tools > Drawing Markups and choose the Pencil tool.

Tip

Sharp-eyed editorial types (like you) might spend way too much time trying to sort out the difference between Drawing and Drawing Markup(s) in various places they appear in the Acrobat menu options. In version 7.0, there's both a Drawing toolbar and a Drawing Markups toolbar, and there are Drawing tools and Drawing Markup (singular) tools. We have no idea what distinction these different labels were meant to, um, draw, but don't worry about it. You can find the Pencil tool under anything that includes "Drawing."

2. Use your mouse to make editorial marks on the PDF page.

We carry natural dog food, natural dog diets--preservative free and dogs, natural nutrition for cats.

3. To "erase" any of these marks, use the Pencil Eraser tool that appears right next to the Pencil tool. It works pretty much like the pink rubber end on a yellow number 2.

Advantages: You can use this tool to draw simple proofreading marks; for example, to note changes for capitalization, inserting periods, deleting spaces and hyphens, and any other uncomplicated, easily recognized edit. Those who are accustomed to seeing standard editorial marks on hard copy might prefer to see them in a PDF file, too.

Disadvantage: You must have an exceptionally steady hand to use this tool; otherwise, the marks can look pretty ragged (as they do in our sample). Also, this can be a time-consuming way to mark changes.

T i p

Some people like to use different Acrobat tools for different types of edits in a PDF document. For instance, they might use the Pencil tool for marking deletions and insertions and the Note tool for adding queries. Whether you use only one tool or a combination, be sure to indicate in a cover note to the person who will review your work which tool you've used for which type of edits.

Call us (415)-566-2952 for immediate orders and custom requests.

But think hard before you get too free with the tools. Using multiples will slow you down, and despite your cover note, the reviewer could be confused about why you've used which tool when. Also, if you view and/or print your comments (see "Show Comments List" and "Print with Comments Summary" in the next few pages), you'll see/print a list of *every* last insertion, deletion, note, highlight, what have you. Tedious to decipher and a sad sacrifice of trees.

A Few Comments About Comments

Whether you spotlight words in comments with quotation marks, with italics, or by setting them on separate lines, pick just one method and stick to it.

In third bulleted item, change "The" to "the."
or
In third bulleted item, change The *to* the.

or
In third bulleted item, change
The
to
the

The goal of any comment is to make a suggested change perfectly clear, and using a single style in all your comments will help the reviewer understand them quickly and easily. Check with the person who will make the actual changes to find out what comment style he or she would prefer to see.

Viewing Comments

Acrobat lets you sprinkle comments here, there, and everywhere in a document, and when that's done, it lets you line them all up for viewing—order from chaos. To experience it, go to Show Comments List.

Show Comments List. This feature will let you easily scroll through all the comments (yours and anybody else's) in a PDF. When you select this feature, the screen will split horizontally and the comments will appear in the lower pane. You'll see the type of comment (a Note, for example) and who inserted it. Clicking on the text of a comment shown there will take you to the place in the document where that comment was inserted. You can also edit the text of any comment in this listing, and the revised version will appear in the document as well.

Tip
You can see the same display of comments (and work with them the same way) by clicking the Comments tab that appears on the left edge of the page.

Printing

As you've already seen, when editing a PDF file, sometimes it's easier to work with hard copy. The same applies to the comments you've inserted. Luckily, Acrobat lets you print both file and comments and gives you a whole range of options to let you fine-tune the results.

To print your existing file and comments, go to Print with Comments Summary. For more freedom to pick and choose what you print, head for Summarize Comments.

Print with Comments Summary. To select this feature, go to Comments > Print with Comments Summary. When you do, you'll see the Summarize Options dialog box, where you have all kinds of choices.

The first thing to do here, under Choose a Layout, is to decide how you'd like your comments to appear—for example, on the same page as the text or on a separate page.

> **Tip**
>
> If you want to view only certain types of comments or make other changes to the way your comments appear onscreen, you can go to Comments and select Show Comments & Markups. For example, you can choose to show only comments made with the Note tool or only those created by a certain reviewer, or you can choose to hide all comments. But be aware that even if certain comments are "hidden," all comments in the file will print.

In this dialog box, you can also make choices on the paper size for printing, how you'd like your comments sorted (by Author, Page, Date, or Type), as well as the type size of the Comments (Small, Medium, or Large). Be aware, though, that "Small" can be tiny—you may need a magnifying glass to read comments this size.

Be aware, too, that changing the font size can wreak all kinds of havoc, especially when there are several comments on one PDF page (things that fit on one page can now drool onto two, formatting can go haywire, page counts can change—ugly stuff). You may want to leave those font-size buttons alone.

> **Tip**
>
> If you've chosen to place your comments on separate pages, have no fear; the type size of the text in your PDF file won't change. However, if you place the comments and the text on a *single* page and you have several comments on one page of text, your document text may shrink to allow all the comments about it to fit on that page.

Once you've made your choices in the Summarize Options dialog box, click OK and you'll be sent directly to the Print dialog box. As in Word's Print dialog box, you can choose to print all the pages in your PDF or only certain pages.

Summarize Comments. This flexible feature offers you some extremely handy options you don't find in Print with Comments Summary. To select it, go to Comments > Summarize Comments. When you do, you'll see an old friend—the Summarize Options dialog box, with all the same options already discussed. It's only after you've made your choices and clicked OK that you'll see how this feature differs from the previous one.

In Print with Comments Summary, after clicking OK, you're taken directly to the Print dialog box, to print your existing file. In Summarize Comments, after clicking OK, Acrobat creates a *new* file for you to continue to work in, print, or do with what you will.

> **Tip**
>
> If you're planning to print your file with its comments, Summarize Comments can be used much like Print Preview in Word. The new file it creates lets you see how your pages and comments will look.

Creating a File with Selected Pages. To do this, you'll need to "extract" the chosen material.

To pull specific pages from the rest of a PDF file, open the file, go to the Document menu, and select Extract Pages. The dialog box that appears will let you choose the pages—or range of pages—you want to extract. These pages will be placed in a new document. Give it a new file name and save it. Then you can print or send it, as appropriate.

Capturing Certain Selections or Elements. To pull just certain selections or elements—less than a page—from a PDF, go to Tools > Basic > Snapshot Tool or click on the cute little camera icon in the Basic toolbar. You'll get a crosshairs symbol. Holding down your left mouse button, place the crosshairs at one corner of the text or other item you want to capture and move the cursor diagonally to enclose it. When you release the mouse button, a copy of your "snapshot" will be placed on the Clipboard, and from there you can paste it into a new document, for printing or for adding more extensive comments if you wish.

Be aware that the snapshot is an image, just a picture of what appears onscreen at the spot you've selected, so when you paste it into another document, any Comments icons (such as Note) will come along if you've included them in the crosshairs, but only the icon image itself. The text typed in the associated pop-up box is not copied. Sorry.

Some Second-Drawer Tools

In addition to Highlight Text, Note, Pencil, and the printing options, Acrobat contains some other tools you might find handy now and then. All these tools can be found under either Comments or Tools on the main menu bar:

Attach a File as a Comment

With this tool, you can attach an entire file (such as a Word file) as a comment. You can navigate to the file of your choice, select it, then choose an icon (such as a paper clip) to indicate that file on your PDF page. A small yellow icon also appears.

Attaching a file as a comment can be useful if you want to reference a particular report, a style guide, or some other primary source. It can also be a bit cumbersome, so you'll probably want to choose other options when possible.

Upload for Browser-Based Review

Select this option if you want to upload the file to a location where all reviewers can access the file, such as a Web site or file transfer protocol (FTP) site. Acrobat will walk you through the steps.

Tip

For more information on any of the Acrobat Comments tools, look to Comments > How To . . . Comment & Markup. Unlike the dubious assistance you get from Help features in some applications, this item is really useful. We highly recommend it.

Beyond Comments and Tools

In addition to Comments and Tools, Acrobat offers seven menus. Several of them will look familiar to users of Word—or any other Microsoft application, for that matter. And for good reason: they contain many of the same options, which work very much the same as the Microsoft versions.

Consequently, we won't dwell on menus or options that contain nothing new or that aren't especially useful to editors. Instead we'll shine the light on a few Acrobat menus that contain things that are.

Edit

In Acrobat this menu is quite similar to the one in Word, but a few things do bear noting:

Check Spelling. This does exactly what every other spell-checker on the planet does, only less. It hints at *far* more than it delivers. Be aware that it does *not* check the spelling in the vast majority of a PDF file; all it checks are the comments you've inserted. That's it. If you're reading this, Adobe, know that editors and proofreaders everywhere are waiting for you to retool this tool to spell-check *all* the text in a PDF document, not just a few comments.

Find. This tool is a bit better than Check Spelling. A lot better, actually. While it doesn't offer the nuanced options the Word version does, it *will* let you search an entire PDF document (not just the comments) for a word or term.

Search. This is actually closer to the version of Find that appears in Word and to the Search (or Find) feature under your computer's Start menu. With it you can search for items in multiple PDF files, not just a single file. That's a big plus. Of course, because as a rule you can't directly alter the content of a PDF, there is no Replace feature.

Completing Your Work

When you've finished editing the file, whether on hard copy or onscreen, go back and read it (and your comments) again. As we keep saying, when reviewing any piece of writing, it's hard to look for everything at once. That can be especially true when viewing a PDF file. So it's particularly important that you follow the stepwise editing procedure we've outlined in Chapter 2.

Once you've done your final passes, write a cover note, listing any issues or information that pertain to the whole project—such as unresolved questions, the Acrobat tools you've used, how to view your comments, which pages you'll be faxing if you're not sending them all—and return it with the pages or files to whoever has asked you to review them. That way the next person to work on the project will know its exact status and be able to move it right along.

Tip

PDF files are often much larger than Word files, sometimes because of what they have in them, but partially because of the "behind the scenes" formatting of a PDF. Some e-mail programs limit the size of attachments, and a ponderous PDF can make them choke.

To slim down your PDF file before returning it to sender, don't just save it; use the Save As option under File and answer yes when asked if you want to replace the existing file. This optimizes the file and reduces its size. If your file is still too big to tack onto an e-mail message, you might want to consider compressing it (with WinZip, ZipIt, etc.).

Tools

Editing PDFs—a Quick Reference

There's a lot to know about PDF editing. Here's a quick-reference roundup of the highlights.

- ✔ The Acrobat tool most useful to editors is Highlight Text. The Note tool can also be handy.
- ✔ The Pencil tool, and other tools such as Insert Text At Cursor and Cross Out Text for Deletion, let you make marks similar to standard editing marks on hard copy, but they can be difficult and time-consuming to use.
- ✔ Acrobat tools don't toggle on and off as Word tools do. Instead, most tools remain selected until you select another one. If a tool *doesn't* stay selected and you want it to, you can keep it on by choosing Keep Tool Selected under View > Toolbars > Properties Bar.
- ✔ Use Show Comments List for an easy review of all your comments (and those of others) in a file.
- ✔ Use Print with Comments Summary to print comments only, or the current file *and* comments, in different layouts of your choice.
- ✔ Use Summarize Comments to create a new file that incorporates your comments as part of it (for further work) and shows you how your chosen print options will look. Use it, too, if you want to print only

certain portions or elements of your file. You can also print from Summarize Comments once you've made your adjustments.

✔ Acrobat's Find feature is not as comprehensive as the Find feature in Word. The Search feature is more helpful.

✔ When returning your edited file, if you've used multiple tools, include in your cover note which tools you've used for what different purposes.

✔ When e-mailing your edited PDF file, click on Save As and answer yes to the prompt "Replace existing file?" This optimizes the file and reduces its size.

8

PowerPoint Files

True story: We once had a client from Chicago who had a very important presentation to give in London. The presentation relied on ninety-four (!) PowerPoint slides, and the client had put a lot of work into them. The night before the morning presentation, shortly before boarding the transatlantic flight, the client realized the slides were, well, kind of messy. That's when our phone rang.

While the plane was in the air, we scrambled to edit the presentation and, thanks to e-mail, delivered ninety-four clean, consistent slides just as the sun touched the Thames. There are several lessons here:

1. PowerPoint slides are very important to people in business (and in other things).

2. It's easy to introduce error into PowerPoint slides.

3. It's also usually easy to edit them (do the math: ninety-four slides divided by a six-hour flight and one editor).

4. Clients don't always plan ahead.

5. Editors say yes to the darnedest things.

Let's not dwell on 4 and 5, shall we? Let's focus on 3 and the point of this chapter—the smoothest ways to edit PowerPoint slides.

If you've spent any time in conference rooms, you probably are aware that PowerPoint is a widely used application that combines text, graphics, sound, and animation to create presentation materials that can be projected, printed, or shared online.

We won't teach you how to create PowerPoint presentations from scratch, although you'll pick up a bit about that as you learn how to edit them. Which is all to the good, because if you know something about how PowerPoint slides are created, you'll find it easier to correct them. But our real aim is to help you edit them once they're created.

Version alert: The discussion in this chapter is based on the default settings in Microsoft PowerPoint 2003.

Powers You Have and Powers You Don't

Editing in PowerPoint falls somewhere between editing in Microsoft Word, with godlike power to insert, delete, format, and so on, with all changes showing, and editing in Adobe Acrobat, with very limited power to make changes directly and only indirect ways to suggest them (see Chapters 6 and 7).

PowerPoint contains several of the same features you'll find in Word, and using PowerPoint you can easily make direct changes in a slide. But unlike in Word, with its Track Changes feature, you can't show a record of those changes in the slide itself. Nor can you easily insert comments and notes with the flexibility you can in Word and Acrobat, respectively.

Because of this, there are three primary ways you'll be asked to edit Power-Point slides:

- On a hard-copy printout
- In another kind of file (such as a Word file) where the PowerPoint slides have been inserted
- Directly in the PowerPoint file, keeping no record of your changes or keeping one elsewhere

Marking Up Printouts

The most common way to indicate edits to a PowerPoint presentation is to print out the slides and mark on these pages using standard editing/proofreading marks (see Chapter 2), then fax or deliver the pages to the party who will actually change the slides. Here's a recap of things to think about when marking changes on hard copy.

If you're working on hard copy, with printouts of several different slides, number the pages manually if page numbers don't already appear. If you'll be returning your corrections by fax (or not), make sure the changes are very clear and dark. Place any queries directly on the page, not too close to the edge. In fax transmission, material on page edges is sometimes lost or illegible.

If there isn't room to write everything clearly on the printout, create a separate sheet for changes and queries and simply note on the hard copy of the slide where the insertion or change belongs. On the separate changes/queries sheet, clearly indicate the slide to which they apply and the location on the slide where each change belongs. One way to do that is to number the changes and place corresponding numbers on the slide printout.

If it's more convenient, you can also record needed changes on an electronic or printed version of the reporting form described in Chapter 9.

> **T i p**
>
> If a PowerPoint slide has a dark background, you'll be hard-pressed to make your changes visible on the printout. Luckily, if that background was created using a PowerPoint fill color, there's a quick fix: in the Print dialog box, under Color/grayscale, choose Pure Black and White. The background will drop out, the type will print black, and you'll have all the white space you need to mark changes.

Editing Embeds

Sometimes PowerPoint slides are embedded (inserted) in a Word file. If they are, you can edit them in place by double-clicking in the slide and then clicking on the text you'd like to edit. If you do, however, there'll be no record of your changes. If you'd like to create one, you can use Word text to indicate your changes above or below the slide:

The Keys to Customer Service
Care about and believe in:
* Your clients
* Your employees and contractors
* You motto, "How can we help?"

{{In third bulleted item, change "You" to "Your"—Ed.}}

If you insert your PowerPoint edits this way, be sure to set them off in some way from the surrounding text. Highlighting is a great way to do that, as is adding characters (such as the double braces shown here) that are easy to search for because they don't appear elsewhere in the document. To make the note perfectly clear, we've enclosed in quotation marks the specific words being discussed (*You* and *Your*), and ended it with a little signature (—*Ed.*).

You can also insert your notes using Word's Comment feature (see Chapter 6). Just click below the slide, insert a comment, and type away. Because you can't place the comment in the slide itself, it's still a good idea to be very specific in your note about the items that need correction.

However you choose to indicate changes to PowerPoint embeds, be sure whoever will make those changes understands and is comfortable with your system.

The Direct Approach

Many times, no one really cares to track the journey from the original version of a slide to the new, editorially accurate one. Those who will be using the slides just want clean ones. If that's the case, you can make your changes directly in PowerPoint.

There are two ways to do that: the global way and the local way.

The Slide Master. Talk about trickle down; we want one of these for our *life*. The slide master lets you define all kinds of details, then applies them automatically to every slide in a presentation. Using the slide master, you can specify things like type styles for header and body text, bullets, graphical elements, and so on just once, and all the other slides use them—no whining, no arguments. You never have to repeat yourself.

If there's a slide master element that you want to change, go to View > Master > Slide Master. Change it there and you've changed it everywhere.

When you create a new slide for a presentation, text boxes tied to the slide master appear on the page. Always enter your text in these boxes if you can. As long as text is in a slide master text box, you can change its style by changing the style of the slide master.

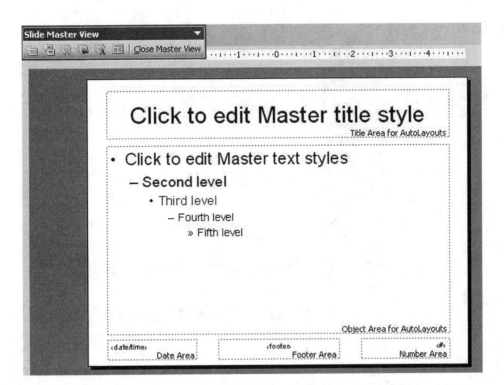

Slide-by-Slide Editing. If global edits aren't an option, you'll have to tackle the slides one by one. PowerPoint offers lots of ways to view and alter them (go to View on the menu bar to see the options). Here are the two we use the most:

Normal View. This view is where you'll do the lion's share of your editing. Here's where you can add and modify text and graphical elements. With a slide in Normal view, click on the header or in the body text and the elements will be surrounded by a bounding box. When that happens, you have the go-ahead to make changes.

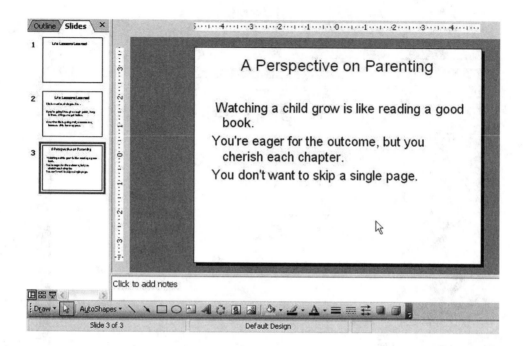

There's more onscreen in Normal view than just the slide you're working on. Those tiny shrunken pages along the left side of the screen are thumbnails of all the slides in the presentation, in the order they appear. Click on them to see the full-size slides and edit them. If you want to change their order, you can just click on a thumbnail, right here in Normal view, and drag it to a different position in the lineup.

There's also a text box, below the slide you're viewing, for notes for the presenter, a built-in speaker's crib sheet. As an editor, you won't often be asked to *add* speaker notes, but you might be asked to review and edit them.

> **Tip**
> Keep in mind that if the presentation will be printed, the speaker notes do not print unless you choose Notes Pages under "Print what:" on the Print dialog.

Slide Show. This view is the PowerPoint equivalent of Word's Print Preview. It lets you step through the entire presentation, slide by slide, to see how it will function and flow. To move from one slide to the next, just click your mouse or tap the down arrow key. To move *back* to a previous slide, use the up arrow key.

In Slide Show view, you see the slides at *full* screen size—no menu bars, no navigation tools, no little icons; nothing but the slide, edge to edge. Editors are rarely asked to verify how well a slide presentation works, but Slide Show does offer you a wide-screen way to do a final review of your work.

Tip

So if no tools are visible in Slide Show, not even the little X in the upper right corner, how do you get *out* of Slide Show view? That one stymies most first-time users. Easy answer: press the Esc key.

Objects from Elsewhere. As we noted above, PowerPoint slides can be embedded in files of different applications. The opposite is also true; sometimes elements from Microsoft Word and Excel (text, tables, graphs, etc.) are inserted into a PowerPoint file. You can't edit these visitors directly in PowerPoint, but you can *open* them directly from PowerPoint into the program in which they were originally created (e.g., Word or Excel). Then you can edit them just as you would if they'd never left home.

To return one of these objects to its birthplace, right-click on it and, from the drop-down menu that appears, select Document Object > Open. That opens the object fully inside Word or Excel. When you have completed your edits in the original application, close the file and you and your changed object will be returned to PowerPoint. Pretty slick.

Save your changes to the PowerPoint file the same way you do in other Microsoft applications, and don't forget to save often.

PowerPoint Graphs. You don't have to use Word or Excel to create graphs for a PowerPoint presentation; you can do it right in PowerPoint. If you want to make edits to a PowerPoint graph, double-click on the graph. This will launch the Microsoft Graph application from within PowerPoint. Along with the editable graph object, a spreadsheet will appear (where you can make data edits).

Tip

Here's something that drives us crazy: Using a drawing tool, you make a nice, neat connector line between two related items and then change one little thing somewhere else on the slide (or the page). Suddenly, your line goes to nowhere—or to somewhere it shouldn't. Arrgh. Here's how to prevent that from happening.

To keep certain objects grouped together, no matter what else moves around, hold down the Shift key while you click on the various objects you want to group. Then click the Draw button on the Drawing toolbar at the bottom of the slide. From the pop-up menu that appears, select Group. It's a great stress reducer.

Inserting Comments and Recording Changes in PowerPoint

Sometimes, time-consuming and often cumbersome as it is, you'll be asked to create a record of the changes you made directly to the PowerPoint slides. When that's the case, you have a few options:

✔ **You can record them on a ready-made electronic reporting form.** This can be an efficient way to itemize corrections. (See Chapter 9 for more information and a sample.)

✔ **You can type your changes and queries into the Notes section of each slide.** See the sample electronic reporting form for ideas on how to word your changes. The key is to describe very clearly the change you made and indicate exactly where you made it. One caution: using this method, you must be sure to distinguish your remarks from those that are actually a part of the presentation (perhaps by highlighting your notes).

✔ **You can use the Insert Comment feature to record your changes.** Similar to the reviewing feature in Word, you can search for, add to, edit, or delete your comments when you display the Reviewing toolbar. Other helpful hints: you can view all comments by displaying the Revisions toolbar, and you can print your comments (see next section).

PowerPoint Printing

Printing in PowerPoint is no different from printing in most other Microsoft applications—you've got options aplenty and choices to make. Most will look familiar to you if you've printed in Word, but there are a couple of PowerPoint-peculiar printing options it's helpful to understand.

In the lower left corner of the Print dialog box, you'll see a drop-down menu under "Print what:". From that menu you can choose, for example, Slides to print each page individually or Handouts to print thumbnails of multiple slides on one page.

In the menu just below that you have the option to print Color, Grayscale, or Pure Black and White. Sometimes the page will print more clearly in one mode than in another—you may need to experiment.

And to print any comments you've inserted in the slides, check the "Print comments and ink markup" option.

Tools

PowerPoint Editing—a Quick Reference

For easy review, here are the highlights of PowerPoint editing:

- ✔ If you edit on printouts, keep changes clear, dark, and away from page edges (for faxing). When printing slides with dark backgrounds, choose Pure Black and White to get an easy-to-mark-on white background instead.
- ✔ If you edit a PowerPoint slide embedded in a Word file, you can create a record of your work by indicating any changes or comments above or below the slide.
- ✔ If you edit in PowerPoint, you'll have no record of your changes, unless you keep one elsewhere (such as on a reporting form, in the Notes section, or by inserting Comments). When making changes in PowerPoint:
  - Use the slide master for editing certain global elements, such as type styles and bullets.

- Edit specific text in individual slides.
- Normal view is the best choice for most editing tasks and for rearranging the slide order. Slide Show view can be helpful, too.
- To edit objects included from applications like Word and Excel, open them from PowerPoint into their original application, make changes, then close them to return the edited version to PowerPoint.

9

Web Sites

Every minute of every day, more and more words appear on the Web. It's easy—almost too easy—to publish online, yet Web pages need the same scrutiny as pages that come between covers; in fact, they need more. Why?

Where Language Goes, Rules Follow

First, e-mail and text messages notwithstanding, the rules of writing really do reach into cyberspace. Readers can be just as confused by a misplaced comma or a tangled transition on a Web page as on a book page. And because speed is often paramount in posting on the Web, errors born of haste are all the more likely. So an editorial eye becomes that much more necessary for Web content, for both the reader's sake and the author's image.

Links, Banners, Buttons, and Bars

Second, Web pages have things book pages do not, and those things need to look right and work correctly. The functional and interactive elements that appear on Web pages need to be checked and verified every bit as much as the words that go with them and for the same reasons—to prevent confusion, frustration, and misunderstanding. Doing so is what makes editing or proofreading for the Web a special task.

Real Marks for Virtual Pages

You can't mark changes directly on a Web page, but that doesn't mean errors need escape. There are several ways to catch and correct them, some fairly low-tech, and some a bit higher. When working with Web pages, you can do some things offline and others with an Internet connection.

To test and verify interactive elements, you'll naturally need to view them online. You can pick up errors in text and note changes to it while viewing it "live" too, but you don't have to. For text, there are alternatives.

For instance, you can make a hard-copy printout of a Web page and mark corrections manually. Or, using an application like SnagIt, you can capture a screen and insert it in another file, such as a Word, PDF, or PowerPoint file, and use many of the editing tools supplied by those applications.

With this range of options, you'll probably note editorial changes—whether they apply to text or to interactive elements—in one of three ways:

- On a hard-copy printout of the page
- On a separate electronic reporting form
- In an electronic file created from a screen capture

A few pointers about each of these methods will help you handle Web pages smoothly and efficiently, however you review them.

Marking Changes on Hard Copy

If you're working on hard copy, with printouts of several different screens, be sure to number the pages manually if page numbers don't already appear. You'll often return your corrections by fax, so mark changes very clearly, using standard editorial marks (see Chapter 2 for samples). Place any queries directly on the page, not too close to the edge. In fax transmission, material on page edges is sometimes lost or illegible.

If there isn't room to write everything clearly on the printout, create a separate sheet for changes and queries and simply note on the hard copy of the Web page where the insertion or change belongs. On the separate changes/queries sheet, clearly indicate the Web page to which they apply and the location on the page where each change belongs. One way to do that is to number the changes and place corresponding numbers on the Web page printout.

If you want to, you can also record needed changes on an electronic or printed-out reporting form.

Using an Electronic Reporting Form

Sometimes clients prefer to receive changes and queries via e-mail, rather than on hard-copy printouts of Web pages. When they do, an electronic reporting form (like the one at the end of this chapter) can be a real convenience.

When reporting needed changes on an electronic form, it's vital to clearly indicate both the exact change to be made *and* the location of each change. Include the name of the page or a page identifier. And if you're using page numbers as identifiers, be sure everyone working on the project agrees about what a "page" is. Sometimes authors and Web developers define them differently. If no other identification method is specified, use the page's address (its URL), which is located on the address bar of your Web browser. If the address bar isn't showing, make it visible using the menu options on your browser's toolbar (in Internet Explorer, View > Toolbars > Address Bar).

Then specify the paragraph and line, but keep in mind that on different computer screens the lines may display differently. To avoid confusion, instead of saying, for example, "p. 4, line 3, delete *the*," you might say, "p. 4, line 3, change *look at the him* to *look at him*."

If you find the same error appearing on several screens, you can enter the needed change just once on the form, the first time you note the error, then copy and paste the change into all other appropriate spots on the form.

Tip

To make the reporting form (a Word file) easily accessible as you work, minimize it and keep it a click away at the bottom of your screen.

Using a Screen Capture

When using a screen capture application such as SnagIt, you can easily capture an entire Web page (what is showing on the screen and even what is not showing), or you can capture any element of any size on the page—text or art. You can even capture pages that scroll.

You then have the choice of printing out the screen captures and marking your changes on the hard-copy printouts. Or, as we mentioned earlier, you can insert the captures into another application, such as Word, Acrobat, or PowerPoint. At *that* point you can use the editing tools those applications contain to comment on the screen capture. Note we don't say *mark up* the screen capture; screen captures may contain words, but they're treated as images and cannot be edited directly.

If you will be returning changes electronically, be sure the file that contains your corrections is named to accurately describe the page you're commenting on, using either a specified locator method or the URL of the page, as noted earlier.

Tip

As in any editorial task, it's very helpful to review Web pages in stages—text first, then other elements, one by one. If you look at all headings, all navigation buttons, all banners, etc., in isolation, you'll be far less likely to become distracted or miss things. (For more on helpful editorial procedures, see Chapter 2.)

What to Watch for on the Web

Elsewhere in this book we've discussed what to look for as you review general text. All that applies to Web text too. Words need to communicate effectively, wherever they appear. So the 3 Cs covered in Part Two—Is It Correct?, Is It Consistent?, Is It Clear (and Compelling)?—all apply to Web text as much as they do to any other writing. But in Web content a few of them need extra attention:

Is It Correct?

There's correct, and then there's correct on the Web. Heads up for:

Punctuation. In particular, pay close attention to em dashes, en dashes, hyphens, apostrophes, and quotation marks. These don't always convert correctly from a word processing program into Web content. With the improvement of conversion software, this isn't as big a problem as it used to be, but these marks—as well as symbols such as mathematical operators, degree symbols, and so on—often appear incorrectly or are dropped altogether. Keep an eagle eye out for them.

Tip

In the world of word processing, apostrophes and quotation marks can be curly (smart) or straight (not dumb, exactly, just noncommittal). In Web materials especially, you often see both styles in the same document. Stay alert to be sure these tiny marks are *all* either Mensa material or average Joes.

Figures, Graphs, and Art. If text was originally written to appear in print materials, "location" terms may have been used that don't apply in Web content, such as "See the graph at left" or "the table on page 62." If all the content is freshly minted for the Web, and none of it was imported from other applications, you shouldn't see locators like these. But if any bits or pieces came from other sources, some inappropriate locator terms may remain. Until *you* read it, that is.

Web Links. Obviously, you'll find many more Web links in Web content than in other electronic copy. You or someone else should click every single link to make sure it does what—or goes where—it should.

As you check links, keep in mind what linked text to review and what linked text *not* to. Links may be to pages or elements within the project you're reviewing, and those probably are your responsibility. But links may also be to any other location on the Web, and it's not your job to proofread all of cyberspace. Be sure you're clear on which part of it you *are* responsible for.

> **Tip**
> Every time you review a page, check tables of contents and indexes. Why? It's easy when adding or deleting content to forget to change their associated links.

Is It Consistent?

Normally, consistency is a cornerstone of effective writing. In most writing, style that varies serves only to confuse. But on the Web, there's an area where style gets a freer rein, with no harm done: e-learning, including online quizzes.

Web content in general and online courses in particular often have multiple authors. So do print learning materials, but in e-learning content it can seem like a cast of thousands.

An e-learning site, for example, might have courses on many topics, each written by a collection of different authors, possibly edited by different instructional designers and reviewed again by subject matter experts. Those are a lot of cooks for the e-learning stew. It's a little unrealistic to make them all toe the same stylistic line.

If you're checking e-learning courses or any other kind of online quizzes or exercises for consistency, you'll probably need to make some things uniform but be able to let some things go. To find out which are which, be sure to check with whoever has asked you to do the work.

For example, a client may want to make sure that ranges of dates always contain an en dash, not a hyphen (*2003–2005*, not *2003-2005*), but may not be concerned if one author says *the thirties* and another says *the '30s*. Or the client may not be concerned if one author writes in active voice and another writes in passive voice. Keep detailed notes about these items on your style sheet.

Is It Clear (and Compelling)?

Like any other text, Web content needs to be clear, but what's considered clear on the Web is sometimes different from what's considered clear in more strait-laced places.

People who write Web copy presume that readers of online content want things faster, shorter, and sometimes more casually presented—much like advertising copy. Shortened or abbreviated phrasing that you might query in a book or manual might be just fine (or preferable) for an online venue.

> **Formal:** *Take $50 off two or more CD towers. It's pricing that gives you more for less.*

> **Informal/casual:** *Take $50 off two or more CD towers. More-for-Less pricing.*

If casual is the consistent style of the writing, go with the flow and don't try to force the material into a more academic or formal style. At the same time, as always, if you ever feel that text is confusing, awkward, ambiguous, or just doesn't make sense, be sure to query it; or, if you're working beyond the level of proofreading, suggest changes as appropriate.

Although many Web writers use a casual or shortened style, they (and you) need to remember something important: if you're writing for the Web, you're writing for a global audience. The Internet is blind to borders, and if content is online, anyone, anywhere, can access it. And when they do, even if they speak English, they might be stumped by American slang or shorthand phrasing. Writers and editors for the Web need to keep in mind that *any* kind of casual phrasing, humor, slang, or other nonstandard writing runs the risk of confusing global audiences. (See "Writing for the World" in Chapter 5 for more.)

Shortened with slang: *We're on call 24/7.* ("On call" may not be understood everywhere, and a slash does not mean the same thing in different languages.)

Globally understood or easily translated: *We're available anytime you telephone or e-mail.*

Substitute standard phrasing for slang or abbreviations, or, if it's not your job to "fix" content, and you find text you think might stymie a global audience, either contact the client/author to ask if he or she would like you to note places you think might be changed, or include your thoughts in a cover note instead of marking the changes or adding queries in the document.

Does It Work?

In reviewing Web content, this is a subject that takes off into new editorial territory; the checklist at the end of this chapter will guide you through it. It goes far beyond the 3 Cs to address the way a Web page looks and works. Although not all-inclusive, the checklist covers the main areas to watch while reviewing the function of a Web page, as well as some tasks beyond the scope of most editing or proofreading. Those extra items would normally be considered QA (quality assurance) tasks. But when budgets are tight, editors are often asked to do double duty and may wind up reviewing some QA items, so we've included them.

Most of what appears in the Checklist for Web Editing is self-explanatory, but some areas merit a little discussion:

Browser Testing. Sometimes it seems as if computer components and software stay current for minutes rather than months or years. Blink, and a new version is available. Web browsers may have a little better shelf life, but only a little. People change and update their browsers constantly.

That means it's important to verify that the Web content you're reviewing appears as it was meant to in a variety of browsers and a variety of versions. It's not always the responsibility of the proofreader or editor to test Web material in different browsers, but if you're asked to do it and you have the technology, Web surfers everywhere will thank you.

For PC people, Internet Explorer is the most-used browser, although Netscape has its fans. For Mac users, Safari is the leader, followed by Firefox. If you have different browsers available, opening Web pages in them may alert you to features that work in one but not another. With luck, your pages will work beautifully in all of them. If they don't, note what works differently from browser to browser. Fixing these items may involve nothing more than the developer or Webmaster tweaking a bit of code.

Content Text. In addition to watching for details—such as punctuation marks—that don't convert accurately to the Web, pay close attention to the placement of text on the page. Graphics can end up obscuring text.

> ### T i p
>
> Always review a Web page at full size, making sure it fills your whole screen. Sometimes text is obscured only because the page is reduced so much there isn't room for all the text to show. The default display size (small or large) for text in your browser can also affect how Web items display. If features or text on the page overlap or display incompletely, try a different type size setting before assuming the problem lies with the page. (To reset the type size, go to View > Text Size.)

Downloads. Many Web sites give the reader an opportunity to download software and additional material (often as PDF files). As a rule, the editor or proofreader is expected to make sure the download takes the reader to the correct download location—but is *not* responsible (as mentioned earlier, under "Web Links") for proofreading the downloads themselves. It's a good idea to verify this with your client, however. Remember one of the golden rules of any kind of editing: *Never assume.*

Dynamic and Interactive Features. These are the things on the Web that grab your attention or give you something to do with your mouse besides scroll. There are so many of them, nudging you for notice, that they could fill a book by themselves. So let's define some terms:

- **Static text** is text that doesn't move—like the words on this page.
- **Dynamic text or graphics** do move. These could be pictures that rotate, animations, and so on. Dynamic text may move, but the user has no control over it and does not affect it in any way.
- **Interactive features** are those the user has some control over or can manipulate to get a response.

A Help menu is one simple example of an interactive feature. When you ask a question within a Help feature, such as how to format a table, it comes back with instructions or options for you, based on what you asked.

Another example is a multiple-choice online quiz. You are generally asked a question (*What's the longest river in Uganda?*), and based on the answer you choose, you may get feedback in the form of test results or further instructions. (*Answer: the Nile. A piece of it starts in Uganda.*)

Dynamic Elements. To review these moving targets, be careful to wait until their entire sequence is completed, more than once, to be sure you've seen everything. You may need to view it many times to make sure you're seeing every word, in context, in the order it's intended to be seen. This can be tricky, so stay extra focused.

> **T i p**
>
> Don't click twice on an interactive object; it may interpret the second click as a second command and repeat whatever it is supposed to do. If you're tempted to click again because the element loads sluggishly, note in your comments that it's slow.

Sometimes moving text will sequence only once. Sometimes the text goes through a rotation of, say, two or three phrases and then stops. In that case, refresh the image and the rotation should start over. Keep track of each change by counting iterations, location, wording, or anything else that applies, so if you need to specify a change, you can note which "version" of the onscreen element the change applies to. Also, be careful to click all More and Next buttons and follow every link to be sure you see all the content there is.

Interactive Features. Some of the most challenging interactive features to check for anomalies are the tests and exercises that come with online learning materials. There are many different types of interactive exercises, but multiple choice with a single correct answer, multiple choice with multiple correct answers, drag-and-drop, and fill-in-the-blank exercises are the ones you see most often. When reviewing these features, be sure you know how many correct answers are intended for each question and what feedback is expected for each right and wrong answer.

For example, sometimes the feedback for all incorrect answers is the same. Sometimes there is different copy for each incorrect answer, containing an explanation of why the incorrect choice is wrong—or not preferred.

> **Tip**
>
> When proofreading online quiz results, you may need to turn off the scoring feature so you can see the feedback for all possible answers.

Graphics. In addition to ensuring the editorial accuracy of any words that appear in graphics on the Web pages, take the time to look at the graphics as a user would. Make sure the graphics appear as intended, in the order intended, and that none are cut off, blocking text, or blocked by text.

Page Titles. The not-terribly-riveting titles of Web pages (e.g., *cs-edit.com/what we do/html*) show up in the browser address bar. While it's not usually your job to confirm that these accurately reflect the page you're viewing, we don't know of a single client who would mind if you did so. Today, Web page titles are often generated automatically, but it doesn't hurt—nor does it take long—to make sure they are correct.

Screen Resolution. Reviewing pages at different screen resolutions is not usually something editors and proofreaders are asked to do—unless they've taken on that QA role. In a Windows system, to check a page at different screen resolutions, go to the Start menu > Control Panel > Display > Settings and adjust the screen resolution (number of pixels by number of pixels).

> **Tip**
>
> Be aware that different text and screen sizes, as well as different resolutions, affect the way text appears on a Web page.
>
> With smaller screens, lower resolutions, or larger text sizes, you may have to scroll around to see everything. That might be confusing—or risky. Also, the relationship of elements on the page can get squeezed or stretched or otherwise changed. Not good if the text reads "In the graphic to the right,"

and the graphic actually appears *under* the statement. If you're reviewing a page at different text sizes or resolutions or on different screens, make note of any such potential problems.

Tools

Sample Electronic Reporting Form

Using a form like this, you can note editorial changes to Web pages while viewing them onscreen and then e-mail the list of changes to whoever has asked for your comments. Use this form if it suits or customize it for your own project. We've filled in some sample information here. (**Note:** The color highlights on this form appear gray on this page only.)

Sample Electronic Reporting Form

Proofreader:	Karen Mead
QA Reviewer:	K.D. Sullivan
Date:	3-14-06
Web Site	www.cs-edit.com

NOTE: First-review queries highlighted in aqua; second-review queries in green.

Page Locator	Change/Query Location	OK	Change/Query Details
Home	para 1, line 2		Add a hyphen to ***self-discovery***
Contact	Main page	X	
Contact	Top-right pop-up, line 3		Change ***everyday*** to ***every day*** (two words)
Services		X	
Press Releases		X	
Company	Photo caption		P1, l2: Change ***an end*** to ***this end***?
Curriculum	Left side, question 4		1. Delete ***The*** and capitalize the ***s*** on ***sentences*** 2. Add a period at the end
Curriculum	Right side, answer 4		1. Delete ***The*** and capitalize the ***s*** on ***sentences*** 2. Add a period at the end
http://sitemap/TERMS/dynamic	Definition of *dynamic*, line 1		Add a period after ***changes***
Registration	All		Screen is blank except for a scroll bar

Checklist for Web Editing

Use this checklist (in *addition* to the complete editorial checklist in Appendix B) to be sure Web page text is error free and Web page function is flawless.

Checklist for Web Editing	✔ First Reading	✔ Second Reading
Browser Testing (for QA Review)		
• In both Internet Explorer and Netscape, and in Safari or another Mac-based Web browser:		
-Layout and text positioning are correct.	☐	☐
-Graphics align properly.	☐	☐
-There are no other browser-specific anomalies.	☐	☐
Content Text		
• No inappropriate or extraneous characters display (e.g., ampersands and other HTML code, or boxes in place of intended characters).	☐	☐
• No text overlaps a background image or a graphic.	☐	☐
• All text wraps correctly and there are no incorrect line breaks.	☐	☐
Downloads		
• Any links to download files or browser plug-ins (e.g., Macromedia Flash) work properly and allow easy return to the site.	☐	☐
Dynamic and Interactive Features		
• Pop-ups, moving banners, and "rotating" text are accurate, and all have been viewed.	☐	☐
• Methods are included to download and install any needed plug-ins, such as Macromedia Flash.	☐	☐
• In online quizzes, all possible answers, when selected, trigger appropriate answer feedback.	☐	☐
• Any write-on lines (WOLs) are the correct length.	☐	☐
• All keypress instructions, when executed, produce the correct result.	☐	☐
• Keypad and upper keyboard numbers work interchangeably.	☐	☐
Graphics		
• All graphics load properly.	☐	☐
• All graphics load promptly.	☐	☐
• All graphics display correctly.	☐	☐
Links		
• There are no "dead" or broken links.	☐	☐
• There are no "too slow" links.	☐	☐
• If a link opens a new browser window, it's easy to return to the main page.	☐	☐
Navigation (for QA Review)		
• All navigation buttons, such as Next and Previous, work properly.	☐	☐
• The navigation interface is easy to understand and follow.	☐	☐
• If navigation is via graphical elements (like buttons) rather than text links, there is an alternative hypertext navigation menu for use should the graphic fail to load.	☐	☐
• After navigating to subpages, the user can always return to the original page.	☐	☐

Checklist for Web Editing *(continued)*	✔ First Reading	✔ Second Reading
Page Titles		
• The correct title for each page appears in the browser title bar window.	☐	☐
Screen Resolution (for QA Review)		
• The site works properly at different screen resolution settings (e.g., 800 x 600, 1024 x 768, and higher).	☐	☐
Scrolling		
• Appropriate scroll bars appear on each page that scrolls.	☐	☐
• No scroll bars appear when a page fits on one screen.	☐	☐
• Unless the site is designed to pan horizontally, there is no horizontal scrolling.	☐	☐

Appendix A

Specialty Editing

In many ways, editorial review is editorial review, no matter what the writing is about. Whether the subject is botany or brake repair, investing or interstellar space, your objective is always the same—to ensure that the finished product is correct, consistent, and clear. And the stepwise procedures you use to reach that goal (see Chapter 2) shouldn't vary.

That said, it's also true that each industry, each client, and each project has its own nuances. There are literally hundreds of editorial specialty areas that have their own peculiarities and requirements, and familiarity with their quirks makes meeting their needs much easier.

To that end, we'll offer tips on four areas: advertising, annual reports with financials, catalog copy, and computer-related text.

Special Topics, Not Special Skills

Don't think that because you don't have expertise in a particular field you can't edit material for it. With the guidelines in this book, your general editorial experience, and a good style sheet or two, you have what it takes to do a very capable review.

Also, in reading any material, you begin to see *patterns*, and you quickly notice when something doesn't quite fit that pattern. For example, if in computer-related text you repeatedly see "Click on the OK button" and "Click on the Next button," and suddenly you see "*Press* the OK button," you know you've got an inconsistency on your hands that requires a change or a query.

Still, in specialty editing you might need to let go of some things you'd ordinarily mark or change in general text. Particular professions, industries, and projects often have reasons to use language in ways that don't conform to *Chicago* and *Webster's,* and you need to be sensitive to that. In specialty editing, it's important to be alert to, and respectful of, the style conventions of that specialty.

Advertising

Advertising copy comes in many forms—letters, brochures, posters, sale coupons, buckslips (one or more small inserts—about the size of a dollar bill—included with a letter or brochure), print ads, Web copy, point-of-sale (POS) pieces like banners and table displays, billboards, even press releases.

Advertising Style—a Whole Different Animal

In advertising copy, as in Web copy, it's safe to assume that readers want things faster, shorter, and sometimes more casually presented. Shortened or abbreviated phrasing that you might query in a book or manual might be just fine (or preferable) for ad copy. If the writing is consistently casual, don't try to make it more formal. Just make sure it's clear. As always, if any text strikes you as confusing, awkward, or ambiguous, or it just doesn't make sense to you, be sure to query it, or if you're working beyond the level of proofreading, suggest appropriate changes.

> **Tip**
>
> Some clients use different styles for different media. For example, they may use en dashes in ranges of numbers in print ads, but use hyphens in Web copy. To be in touch with small differences such as these requires good communication with your clients, as well as a good style sheet.

Some style choices made for advertising copy may seem just plain wrong to editors, but the reasons behind them can be compelling.

Does anyone remember the furniture polish ad campaign with the slogan "Treats Wood Good"? To the grammatically sensitive, that was fingernails on a blackboard. But even your English teacher would have to admit that "Treats Wood Well" wouldn't have been nearly as catchy. Who knows? Maybe part of what made the slogan stick was the obvious misuse of *good.* So was the slogan wrong? Grammatically, yes; from a business standpoint, probably not (we don't know the sales figures). In any event, the wording was someone's conscious choice and not subject to editing.

Another example comes from Toyota. Several years ago the company had a TV campaign with the slogan "Toyota Everyday." Again, fingernails on a blackboard to those who know this should be "Toyota Every Day." (Adverb, not adjective form.) In hopes they would hire her to save them future grammatical embarrassment, K.D. tracked down Toyota's U.S. marketing manager to point out the error.

It turns out that Toyota had done extensive research before choosing the wording and determined that people just seemed to like *everyday* better than *every day*. How do you argue with that? In advertising, it's all about appealing to potential customers, most of whom aren't grammarians. (By the way, the call wasn't a complete waste of time; K.D. did get a referral for her efforts.)

The moral here is to take your cue from industry styles and from your client or the company you work for. Rely on style sheets if an advertising agency has one (or several), and as always, if they don't, be sure to create them.

Following style guidelines for an ad agency can be more of a challenge than following the style of one company—because the agency often has several clients of its own, all with different styles. And some have multiple clients in the same industry—each with its own focus and styles.

For instance, one advertising agency we know had three different clients who all worked in the health-care industry. Each had its own way of referring to the profession:

Client A	*health care* (n),	*healthcare* (adj)
Client B	*health care* (n),	*health-care* (adj)
Client C	*healthcare* (n),	*healthcare* (adj)

Just another reason to cherish your style sheet(s).

Tip

In all editorial review, but especially when working in specialized fields, don't be frustrated or take offense if a client rejects a suggestion you've made. As you've seen, clients have their own valid reasons for the choices they make. It's your job to mark changes and make suggestions, but it's up to the client to take them or leave them.

Trademark Symbols

The purpose of advertising copy is to promote something, and that something is often protected by a trademark. When a brand or product name appears in general (not advertising) text, an initial capital letter is enough to signal its special status. But in advertising and promotional materials, a small symbol often follows the name.

By law, trademark and other symbols don't *have* to appear to ensure protection, but most people in advertising choose to include them. That tiny ® or ™ speaks volumes about hard work, creativity, and ownership. (For a rundown of all the marks and what each one means, go to the Web sites of the U.S. Patent and Trademark Office and the International Trademark Association.)

Here are some things to keep in mind when working with proprietary terms:

- Never assume a brand or product name is generic. If you are unsure, query your client or check on the United States Patent and Trademark Office or International Trademark Association Web site.
- Whether using symbols or not, always distinguish trademarked terms in some way, such as with an initial capital letter or with boldface or italic type.
- Use only the proper, trademarked form of the term wherever it appears.
- In general, use a trademark as an adjective modifying a noun (*a Xerox copy*), not as a noun (*I have a Xerox of that*) or a verb (*I need to Xerox that*).
- Any symbol used should directly follow the trademarked term (or logo).
- The ® or ™ symbol need appear in only the first or most prominent mention of a trademarked item. Some prefer to use it in the title of a document, but many prefer to use it when the item is first mentioned in the text.
- A single reference to the trademark (such as to which company the trademark is registered) is sufficient within the document. If the trademark is used in sections of a document that may be distributed separately, the symbol and a reference should be used in each.
- Symbols are used online the same as they are in printed works.

Tip

Many companies include product and brand names—with any relevant symbols—on their style sheets. If you aren't supplied with this information, be sure to ask for it, and if no list exists, start one yourself, for the client to verify.

Annual Reports with Financials

Annual reports usually have three parts: a letter from the CEO or a letter to the shareholders, the text of the report, and the financial information.

JOHNSON LUMBER

Condensed Statement of Operations
(in millions)

	Three Months Ended		Nine Months Ended	
	June 30, 2006	June 30, 2005	June 30, 2006	June 30, 2005
Net sales	$ 3,468	$ 2,108	$ 9,983	$ 8,914
Cost of sales	2,214	1,220	7,452	6,890
Gross margin	1,254	888	2,531	2,024
Operating expenses:				
Research and development	125	108	387	367
General and administrative	375	306	973	927
Marketing & Sales Division	95	62	286	210
Total operating expenses	595	476	1,646	1,504
Operating income	659	412	885	520
Other income and expense:				
Interest and other income, net	45	12	87	38
Total other income and expense	45	12	87	38
Income before provision for income taxes	704	424	972	558
Provision for income taxes	227	135	346	180
Net income	$ 477	$ 289	$ 626	$ 378
Earnings per common share				
Basic	$ 0.57	$ 0.35	$ 0.75	$ 0.45
Diluted	$ 0.55	$ 0.34	$ 0.95	$ 0.43

Most often the letter will be reviewed and the general text prepared by the marketing department (or outsourced to an advertising agency). But the financials are supplied by the financial division. Because these pieces come from different places, you may find style inconsistencies, especially in references to fiscal quarters and years and in abbreviations. For example, you might see:

From the Marketing Dept.
fiscal year 2006
year-end
after-tax dividends
fourth quarter
percent

From the Financial Dept.
FY06, FY 06, FY'06
year end, yr end, YE
after tax dividends
Q4
%

If you're lucky, a style sheet will let you know which of these items should be handled consistently throughout and which ones can be abbreviated in financial charts but should be spelled out in text.

As an editor or proofreader, you aren't responsible for the *accuracy* of the numbers in financial information any more than you're usually responsible for the accuracy of the facts in anything you review. And let's face it, you would probably have no way of knowing which numbers are right and which aren't.

Still, as you do in other types of editing, you can spot certain errors by looking for patterns. This four-step process for reviewing the rows and columns of financials will help you do that:

1. First, read each row from left to right, reading the descriptive text and then the numbers. Pay attention to whether any entries in the numbers columns seem out of place. You wouldn't bat an eye, for example, if under "Acquisitions expenditures" 294 appeared for the year 2004 and 1,914 appeared for the year 2005. But if 2004 showed 294 and 2005 showed 1.1%, you'd know something was wrong.

2. Once you've completed your review of each row, read down each column, looking for anything that might be an anomaly and also for proper alignment. Are dollar signs aligned, decimal places aligned, commas in figures placed correctly, etc.?

3. Now go back and read the column of descriptive text from top to bottom. Look to ensure consistency in all things, but especially in spelling, capitalization, and abbreviations. Most lines will be in sentence case (with no ending punctuation), with proper names and department names in title case:

   Boom Bakery profits
   R&D
   Capital expenditures
   Net investment

4. Finally, read the column headings from left to right, looking for the usual—accuracy and consistency in spelling, capitalization, abbreviations, alignment, font, and so on.

T i p

Don't forget to make sure the data is consistent between the text, the financials, and other tables. For example, the introductory text discussing a table might say that fourth-quarter 2005 net earnings were $10.5 billion, but the entry in the table for 2005 Q4 net earnings reads $10.5 *million*. Think of the data—column and row text and the financials—as you would an illustration in regular text and look for consistency in all the same ways—for example, by verifying that captions and numbering match in the text and tables.

Catalogs

In years past, most catalogs were pretty straightforward. They most often had a picture of an item for sale and a title or a brief description of the object, along with pertinent product and ordering information (the old L.L. Bean catalog comes to mind, bless it). And some catalogs are still this "simple."

But today more and more catalogs are glossy marketing pieces that include clever, fun, theme-based descriptions of products, such as this one:

Dorothy Daybed
This daybed does double duty--bright and inviting to sit in the sun with a good book in hand. By night, a firm and comfy bed for a good night's sleep and sweet dreams. Takes standard twin mattress.

DDW619	White
DDR619	Rose
(81"W x 41"L x 46"H)	$159.99

(Pillows shown on page 24.)

Satisfaction Guarantee
We stand behind every product we sell. If for any reason you are not completely satisfied with your purchase, we'll be happy to replace the merchandise or issue a full refund.

1-800-555-0914
HoyerDesign.com

Because of its complexity, you'll need to pay attention to all the same things in catalog text that you would in any other text, and then some.

In catalogs, there are also *lots* of elements you won't normally find in general text. Because there are so many different areas to watch, maintaining consistency in all the ways you usually would is even more challenging.

> **Tip**
>
> Be sure you know which elements your client wants you to review. For instance, one may want all elements, including product number, size, price, etc., verified against copy provided. Others may simply want text proofed and internal consistency of elements verified, with no reference to another source.

Reviewing in stages is extremely important in all editorial work, but in documents with many different elements it's indispensable. Following are some of the elements (in addition to the basic product description) that can accompany a picture of a product. Be sure to look at each element separately to verify accuracy and consistency:

- Product identifiers or product numbers (letters or numbers designating a pictured item and the corresponding description); watch to see that:
  - The picture and description match for a particular product identifier.
  - The placement of product identifier in pictures and in descriptions is consistent.
  - The illustration is of the product described.

Note: Also be sure to check cross-references between pages. Catalogs frequently have photos showing products that are listed and described on another page; for example, "See Tolomeo Desk Lamp on p. 25."

- SKU (Stock Keeping Unit)—a common term for a unique numeric identifier that refers to a specific product in inventory or in a catalog
- Measurements (dimensions and fluid amounts), including decimals, fractions, abbreviations, order of dimensions ($H \times W \times L$)
- Sizes, especially capitalization and the order in which the sizes are listed
- Colors, especially abbreviations, capitalization, and the order in which colors are listed
- Price and special or sale price

- Additional charges, such as for shipping and handling or for oversized or customized objects

Then on certain pages and in certain locations (sometimes as headers and footers) are items such as:

- Toll-free ordering number
- URL
- Ordering information
- Delivery information
- Return policies
- Additional shipping and handling information

More and more, the last four of the preceding are being left for the order form—which you will likely also be reviewing for accuracy and consistency—in the center of the catalog. Some of these still appear, though, as boxed text in the body of the catalog, sometimes on every page or every other page.

Tip

One of the main places that errors slip through in catalog copy is in the description of and ordering information for a product. Clients have a specific order in which items such as product identifiers, SKUs, sizes, dimensions, and so on are to appear. Make verifying this sequence a separate and important stage.

While catalog copy contains more than general text, it can also contain less. Because of space limitations in catalog copy, you'll frequently see—and need to keep consistent, according to style sheet specs—incomplete sentences, abbreviations, or numerals (instead of spelled-out numbers) that might not be appropriate in regular copy.

Computer-Related Text

In computer-related materials, you'll see a lot of copy of that looks like English but isn't. It's a language spoken by computers, and computers are notoriously picky. Most people can overlook a misplaced comma or an extra space; computers can cough on them, or worse.

For that reason, as you tend to the usual editorial tasks in computer-specific text, you'll need to tiptoe very carefully around programming codes, field names, menus, screen elements, and other arcane, high-tech items.

But don't let that daunt you. Computer terminology is just another set of letters and symbols to watch for consistency and to query when they seem amiss. If you follow the guidelines described here and elsewhere in this book, any style guidelines you're given, and the checklist at the end of this chapter, *and* keep an eye out for patterns, you'll do fine.

Just remember one cardinal rule: don't make *any* changes to programming code. Correct the spelling, grammar, and punctuation in the text around it, but never alter the slightest detail in a piece of code. Even moving a period from outside quotation marks to inside or changing the capitalization of a word for "consistency" can cause a computer disaster. Following are examples of how code set off from text might appear:

```
hostname# router 1
```

flash *device:filename*

> **Tip**
> You won't be responsible for verifying the accuracy of programming code, and you probably won't be responsible for verifying the accuracy of URLs (Internet addresses) either. In any event, you should never "edit" them. But you should still *read* them to pick up any obvious typos, like the one in *je-architects .com/draafting*. If you think you spot a typo, query it. And if you edit a lot of computer-related text, you'll be surprised at how quickly you begin to recognize bits of code. Really.

Snippets of code also frequently appear within text, as part of the discussion. Those are off-limits to editors too. You'll be able to pick them out easily enough, because they're usually shown in a font that's different from the surrounding text. Different people choose different styles for them—**bold**, *italic*, and `Courier` are popular choices. Some people use the same font for all code or computer-related elements shown in text; some use a variety of fonts to differentiate different elements, such as:

Arguments (variables)
Arrow keys
Buttons
Character strings
Command names
Command syntax
Dialog boxes
Directory, file, and path names
Drop-downs
Fields
Key names
Keystroke combinations
Keywords
Menus and submenus
Options
Scroll bars
Status bars
Toolbars
User input
Window and screen names

For instance, in a discussion of command syntax (the entire format of a software command), you might see a command in bold and a variable in italics:

{**timeout** *minutes*}

There are so many formatting styles for elements in computer-related content that it can make your head swim. In general text, an editor can rely on *The Chicago Manual of Style*, *The Associated Press Stylebook*, and *Merriam-Webster's Eleventh Collegiate Dictionary*. But there are no hard-and-fast styles or always-deferred-to style references for computer-related text.

You're not entirely on your own, however. *Chicago* and *Webster's* have recently added much more guidance on electronic style and computer terms, the *Microsoft Manual of Style for Technical Publications* (in print and electronic versions) is an excellent reference, and on the Web, Webopedia.com is a great source for computer and Internet technology terms and definitions. Use Google to see how much consensus there is on a term, but don't expect it to show you anything definitive; companies still use a wide variety of styles in computer-related materials, and Google reflects that disparity.

> **Tip**
>
> When a client asks what the "standard" style is for a certain element, when there really is no standard, you might mention that although there aren't any universally accepted styles, you usually see the element a certain way. You might also cite how Microsoft handles certain conventions.

Tools

Checklist for Computer-Related Text

Add this checklist to the complete, three-part editorial checklist in Appendix B to ensure accuracy, consistency, and clarity in computer-related text.

Checklist for Computer-Related Text	✔ First Reading	✔ Second Reading
Graphical User Interface and Screen Elements		
• Text references to graphical user interface (GUI) elements (e.g., menus, icons, dialog boxes, buttons, and toolbars) and onscreen labels and messages are spelled and capitalized as they appear onscreen, unless style guidelines specify otherwise.	☐	☐
• GUI-related verbs (e.g., *check*, *click*, *open*, *close*, *press*, etc.) conform to style guidelines and are used consistently.	☐	☐
Keyboard and Mouse Elements		
• Text references to individual key names (Shift, Tab, etc.) are spelled and capitalized consistently and shown in correct fonts as specified in style guidelines.	☐	☐
• Verbs referring to actions involving the keyboard or the mouse (e.g., *press*, *click*, *double-click*) conform to style guidelines and are used consistently.	☐	☐
Path and File Names		
• Path names and file names are capitalized and punctuated consistently and shown in correct font as specified in style guidelines.	☐	☐
Programming Code		
• No changes of any kind are made to any programming code, in body text, in offset sections, or in art or graphics. Apparent anomalies are *queried only*.	☐	☐
• Within general text, in offset sections, and in art and graphics, specific programming syntax elements (e.g., commands, arguments, character strings, variables, keywords) appear in the correct fonts as specified in style guidelines. Apparent anomalies are *queried only*.	☐	☐
• No punctuation within any programming code is added, deleted, or altered in any way. Apparent anomalies are *queried only*.	☐	☐
• In general text, punctuation (or lack thereof) adjacent to run-in programming code elements conforms to style guidelines.	☐	☐
Software Version Designations		
• Text references to software versions are consistently named and numbered according to style guidelines.	☐	☐

Appendix B

Editorial Extras

For the highly curious or the extra committed, here are a few more editorial tools. You'll find a brief editing test and two different answer keys, some professional-level aids, including a style sheet suitable for professionals (or for people who just want the best), a complete eight-stage proofreading checklist, and an editorial checklist that combines all the topics covered in Part Two. And for your convenience, you'll also find a glossary of some selected terms.

Testing, Testing . . .

Want to gauge your editing skills? Take the following test before reading this book—and then again after, to see how much better you do.

You can use this as an exercise for yourself or to test a potential editor you're considering hiring. And don't worry, we haven't left you hanging. The keys to the test are on pages 200–203. Because editors and proofreaders review at different levels, we've provided two different answer keys, so you'll be able to see the things that should be noted by each. Have fun!

Name _____   E-mail _____

Address _____   Phone _____

_____   Date _____

References Used _____

CSE July 4 Sale—Marketing Proposal and Analysis

After four years of eventful and boistrous Warehouse Sales in the San Francisco bay area, we're pleased to announce our first Warehouse Sale in Hebron Kentucky (near the Cincinnati Airport), on Saturday July 24, Sunday July 26, and Monday July 27. For 2 days only, choose from hundreds of overstocks and near perfect samples —all at up to 30–75% off and more. Delivery services for the surrounding area (Cinncinnati, Columbus, Dayton, Albuquerque and Indianapolis) will be available. Make the trip and show up early for the best selection. And while you're at the sale, enter to win a $1,000 gift certificate.

Store Metrics

The four area locations (store numbers), and percentage of the last July 4 state sales are as follows:

1. Cincinnati (841): 29.7%

2. Columbus (842): 24.3%

3. Dayton (843): 16.1%

4. Louisville (844) 15.3

5. Indianapolis (845): 14.7%

For the time period leading up to and including the July 4 weekend, below are the tim
that showed that highest receipts for the state:

1. 9:00 am–10:00 am (M–F 29.3%)

2. 9:00 am–11 am Saturday (26.8%)

3. 5:00 pm–6:00 pm M–F (20.4%)

Overall, M-F 9:00 a.m.-10:00 a.m. is clearly our strongest timeframe.

Analysis/Stratagy

To improve sales in the weaker times in all markets, we plan to commit $40,000 in
advertising dollars which will be split equally betweent he four stores. As noted by our
C.E.O. "Every store is as important to us as the next".

Ads will be placed in local newspapers to run everyday of the week prior to the
July, 4 weekend. Its been determined that TV and radio is still more effective in bringing
in the desired customers so 75% of the advertising budget will be alocated in these areas.
Spots will run at :05 passed these hours: 9 am; noon; and 5 pm hour.

Our marketing and sales departments marketing plan will be submited for final
approval one week form today.

Testing, Testing . . . Proofreading Answer Key

Note: This answer key is marked at the level of a standard proofread (for more on editorial levels, see Chapters 1 and 5).

CSE July 4 Sale—Marketing Proposal and Analysis

> **Comment [me1]:** Spell out CSE?

After four years of eventful and boisterous warehouse sales in the San Francisco Bay Area, we're pleased to announce our first warehouse sale in Hebron, Kentucky (near the Cincinnati airport), on Saturday, July 24; Sunday, July 26; and Monday, July 27. For three days only, choose from hundreds of overstocks and near-perfect samples—all at up to 30%–75% off and more. Delivery services for the surrounding area (Cincinnati, Columbus, Dayton, Albuquerque, and Indianapolis) will be available. Make the trip and show up early for the best selection. And while you're at the sale, enter to win a $1,000 gift certificate.

> **Comment [me2]:** OK to lowercase "warehouse sales" here and in next line?
> **Deleted:** W
> **Deleted:** S
> **Deleted:** b
> **Deleted:** a
> **Deleted:** W
> **Deleted:** S
> **Comment [me3]:** Sale is on July 4 weekend; pls verify and correct dates.
> **Deleted:** A
> **Deleted:** ,
> **Deleted:** ,
> **Deleted:** 2
> **Deleted:**
> **Deleted:**
> **Deleted:** n
> **Comment [me4]:** Should this be "Louisville," as shown in next section?

Store Metrics

The five area locations (store numbers), and percentages of the last July 4 state sales, are as follows:

> **Comment [me5]:** Change to "location," or edit in some other way? Cities within three states are listed, not states.
> **Deleted:** four

1. Cincinnati (841): 29.7%

2. Columbus (842): 24.3%

3. Dayton (843): 16.1%

4. Louisville (844): 15.3%

5. Indianapolis (845): 14.7%

> **Comment [me6]:** Percentages total 100.1%; pls adjust to total 100%.
> **Deleted:**

For the time period leading up to and including the July 4 weekend, below are the times that showed the highest receipts for the state:

> **Comment [me7]:** Last year's sale took place in three different states; should this be "for these stores"?
> **Deleted:** that

1. 9:00 a.m.–10:00 a.m. Monday–Friday (29.3%)

2. 9:00 a.m.–11 a.m. Saturday (26.8%)

3. 5:00 p.m.–6:00 p.m. Monday–Friday (20.4%)

Overall, Monday–Friday 9:00 a.m.–10:00 a.m. is clearly our strongest time frame.

Analysis/Strategy

To improve sales in the weaker times in all markets, we plan to commit $40,000 in advertising dollars, which will be split equally among the five stores. As noted by our CEO "Every store is as important to us as the next."

Ads will be placed in local newspapers to run every day of the week prior to the July 4 weekend. It's been determined that TV and radio are still the most effective in bringing in the desired customers, so 75% of the advertising budget will be allocated in these areas. Spots will run at :05 past these hours: 9 a.m., noon, and 5 p.m.

Our marketing and sales department's marketing plan will be submitted for final approval one week from today.

| Deleted: M–F |
| Deleted: - |
| Deleted: - |
| Deleted: a |
| Deleted: betweent |
| Deleted: our |
| Deleted: C.E.O. |
| Deleted: . |
| Deleted: , |
| Deleted: is |
| Deleted: passed |
| Deleted: ; |
| Deleted: ; |
| Deleted: hour. |
| **Comment [me8]:** If marketing and sales are two separate departments, pls change to "departments'" and "plans." |
| Deleted: form |

Testing, Testing . . . Editing Answer Key

Note: There are often many different ways to correct and improve a document. This answer key is marked at the level of a medium copyedit (for discussion of editorial levels, see Chapters 1 and 5) and represents just one way, so use it as a guide only.

CSE July 4 Warehouse Sale—Marketing Proposal and Analysis

	Comment [me1]: Spell out CSE?

This ad will be placed in local newspapers to run every day of the week leading up to the July 4 weekend:

> After four years of exciting warehouse sales in the San Francisco Bay Area, CSE is pleased to announce our first warehouse sale in Hebron, Kentucky (near the Cincinnati/Northern Kentucky International Airport), on Saturday, July 24; Sunday, July 26; and Monday, July 27. For three days only, choose from hundreds of overstocks and near-perfect samples—all at 30%–75% off. Delivery services for the surrounding area (Cincinnati, Columbus, Dayton, Albuquerque, and Indianapolis) will be available. Come early for the best selection. And while you're at the sale, enter to win a $1,000 gift certificate.

Comment [me2]: Info here from Analysis/Strategy section: OK? Ad text indented to set off from proposal text.

Comment [me3]: Will ads run *during* weekend as well? If so, pls adjust text.

Deleted: eventful and boistrous

Deleted: W

Deleted: S

Comment [me4]: Change OK? "Eventful and boisterous" might deter some.

Deleted: bay area

Deleted: we're

Comment [me5]: If not spelled out in title, spell out here?

Deleted: W

Deleted: S

Comment [me6]: Correct airport?

Deleted: ,

Comment [me7]: Sale is on July 4 weekend; pls verify and correct dates.

Deleted: ,

Deleted: 2

Comment [me8]: Pls verify and supply highest actual percentage.

Deleted:

Deleted:

Deleted: up to

Deleted: and more

Store Metrics

The five area locations (store numbers) that will participate in the warehouse sale, and their independent percentages of last year's total July 4 area sales, are as follows:

1. Cincinnati (841): 29.7%
2. Columbus (842): 24.3%
3. Dayton (843): 16.1%
4. Louisville (844): 15.3%
5. Indianapolis (845): 14.7%

Comment [me9]: Should this be "Louisville," as shown in next section?

Deleted: n

Comment [me10]: Change for brevity and to downplay inconvenience.

Deleted: four

Comment [me11]: Edits accurate?

Deleted: the

Deleted: state

Comment [me12]: Percentages total 100.1%; pls adjust to total 100%.

Deleted:

For the period leading up to and including the July 4 weekend, below are the times that showed the highest receipts for the state:

1. 9:00 a.m.–10:00 a.m. Monday–Friday (29.3%)
2. 9:00 a.m.–11 a.m. Saturday (26.8%)
3. 5:00 p.m.–6:00 p.m. Monday–Friday (20.4%)

Clearly, our sales are strongest between 9:00 a.m. and 10:00 a.m. Monday through Friday.

Analysis/Strategy

To improve sales in the weaker times in all markets, we plan to commit $40,000 to advertising, which will be split equally among the five stores. As noted by our CEO, "Every store is as important to us as the next."

The print ad that appears at the beginning of this proposal will be placed in local newspapers to run every day of the week prior to the July 4 weekend. However, we have determined that TV and radio are still the most effective in generating business, so 75% of the advertising budget will be allocated in these areas. Spots will run at five minutes past 9 a.m., noon, and 5 p.m.

Our marketing and sales department's complete marketing plan will be submitted for final approval one week from today.

Deleted: time

Comment [me13]: Last year's sale took place in three different states; should this be "for these stores"?

Deleted: that

Deleted: M–F

Deleted: Overall

Deleted: M–F

Deleted: -

Deleted: is clearly our strongest timeframe

Deleted: a

Deleted: in

Deleted: dollars

Deleted: betweent

Deleted: our

Deleted: C.E.O.

Deleted: .

Deleted: Ads

Comment [me14]: Will the ads run *during* weekend? If so, pls adjust text.

Deleted: .

Deleted: Its been

Deleted: is

Deleted: more

Deleted: bringing in the desired customers

Comment [me15]: Specify days and stations on which spots will run?

Deleted: :05

Deleted: passed

Deleted: these hours:

Deleted: ;

Deleted: ;

Deleted: hour.

Comment [me16]: If marketing and sales are two departments, pls change to "departments' complete marketing plans."

Comment [me17]: Correct? Have assumed this proposal is preliminary.

Deleted: form

Expanded/Professional Style Sheet Template

The template that follows is suitable for professional editors or for anyone who wants to ensure the highest level of accuracy in any writing. Choose from the topics on this detailed template to create a customized style sheet for a specific document, a client or department, or an entire organization.

Expanded/Professional Style Sheet Template

Company/Dept./Project: Author(s):

                                          Editor:

Version/Last Update: Proofreader:

Conventions
Note style choices in all applicable categories below.

Capitalization Note capitalization conventions for items (such as department names and lengthy prepositions in titles) that can be treated in different ways.
- In titles and headings:
- In captions:
- Following colons:
- Following em dashes:
- For special terms:

Fonts Note the font types and sizes used for elements that repeat throughout a document.
- Cover sheet/document title:
- Chapter/section titles:
- Body text:
- Text headings:
- Headers:
- Footers:
- Folios (page numbers):
- Captions:
- Tables:
- Table of contents:
- For emphasis:

- For special terms:
- Other:

Headers and Footers Note the content that should appear in headers and footers and how it's positioned (e.g., flush left, flush right, or centered).
- Header content (odd, even, and first page, plus front/back matter):
- Header location (odd, even, and first page):
- Footer content (odd, even, and first page, plus front/back matter):
- Footer location (odd, even, and first page):
- Folio (page number) style (lowercase roman or arabic for front matter):
- Folio location (odd, even, and first page):

Lists Note when a bulleted list is used versus a numbered list, whether all list introductions or only certain ones are followed by a colon, whether all list items begin with a capital letter, if and under what circumstances list items end with punctuation, how list item lead-ins are styled, how lists within lists are handled, and any other list guidelines.
- Bulleted lists:
- Numbered lists:
- List introductions:
- List item capitalization:
- List item punctuation:
- List item lead-ins:
- Lists within lists:
- Other:

Numbers Note which numbers are spelled out and which are shown as numerals; whether commas are used in four-digit numbers; whether even dollar amounts are shown with a decimal and zeros; how numbers are rounded; how percentages are shown; how dates, times, and telephone numbers are formatted; when numbers are used with units of measure; and any other style choices that apply to numbers.
- Spelled-out numbers:
- Numerals:
- Commas in numbers:
- Dollar amounts:
- Rounding:
- Percentages:

continued

- Dates:
- Times:
- Telephone numbers:
- Units of measure:
- Other:

Punctuation Note whether series commas are used; whether there is space or no space around em dashes; how and where other types of dashes are used; whether quotation marks are used around new or specialized terms and whether quotation marks are straight or curly; whether punctuation is used in headings; and any other punctuation style choices.

- Series commas:
- Dashes:
- Quotation marks:
- In headings:
- Other:

Spacing For all copy, note standard number of letter spaces following colons and between sentences. (With a few rare exceptions, such as in some legal or academic works, this should be one space.) For checking formatting as part of copyediting and for proofreading, note page setup parameters, such as margins and indents. Note standard line spacing in body text and around headings and such elements as lists, tables, and captions. Also note justification style (left, center, right, full) as appropriate for all elements.

- Number of spaces following colons and between sentences:
- Margins:
- Indents:
- Body text:
- Above/below headings:
- Above/below lists:
- Above/below tables:
- Above/below captions:
- Justification:
- Other:

Symbols Note whether such things as ampersands, degree symbols, mathematical operator symbols, monetary symbols, and percent signs are used and under what circumstances. If there is a choice of different symbols, be sure to note which one is used.

- Ampersands:
- Degree symbols:
- Mathematical operators:
- Monetary symbols:
- Percent signs:
- Other:

Tables Note all table styles used and the kind of information that should appear in each. In addition to the style (grid lines, shading, etc.) and content type for each style, include formatting parameters such as column widths; text spacing within cells; and capitalization in column headings, left-column row labels, and table cells. Note any special use of abbreviations or numbers in tables.

- Table styles/content:
- Column widths:
- Text spacing:
- Capitalization:
- Abbreviations/numbers:
- Other:

Word Breaks, Widows, and Orphans (for Proofreading) Note any special guidelines for word breaks at the ends of lines in a finished document (e.g., no more than three in a row) and for treatment of widows (a short line at the top of a page) and orphans (a single word or part of a word at the end of a paragraph).

- Word breaks at ends of lines:
- Widows:
- Orphans:

Word List

Include here, in alphabetical order, the exact spelling, capitalization, and font of individual words and terms as they should appear. Include words that can be spelled more than one way, abbreviations and acronyms, hyphenations, proper nouns, proprietary names and terms coined by the author or organization, and any other terms that might need verification by an editor or proofreader. For complex jobs, break this list into categories. For example, Product Names, Trademarked Titles, Module Names, Sample Cases, Contract Provisions, etc.

Professional 8-Stage Proofreading Checklist

The checklist that follows is designed for the professional proofreader, someone already familiar with the technical aspects of proofreading. But it's useful for anyone who wants his or her written materials to be as free of errors as possible.

Not all the items in this list would be considered the proofreader's responsibility if he or she were doing a standard proofread (see Chapter 1 for definitions). However, so often in business, as opposed to traditional publishing, a "proofread" is all a document gets, and the proofreader is asked to review a few items that might otherwise be considered the responsibility of an editor.

In general, a proofreader's focus is on accuracy and consistency, and an editor's focus is on those things as well as on improvement to the writing. An "editorial proofread" falls somewhere in the middle—a bit more than a standard proofread and a bit less than a copyedit. So for the convenience of anyone doing an editorial proofread, we've included in this checklist some of the items that level of work might involve and marked them with asterisks. If you're doing a more traditional standard proofread, you can probably consider these items beyond your job description (but if in doubt, be sure to ask). And if you need to do more than an editorial proofread, use the Complete Editorial Checklist that follows this checklist.

When proofreading, as when editing, to ensure the best finished product, it's vital to go through a piece of writing several times, looking at different elements on each pass (see Chapter 2 for more on the stages of editorial review). The eight stages outlined here, and the items within them, will help you remember not only the process to follow but also the particulars to look for as you work.

Professional 8-Stage Proofreading Checklist	✔ First Reading	✔ Second Reading

Stage 1: Body Text

Before You Begin
- Review or set up a style sheet.   ☐ ☐

Sense, Clarity, and Flow
- Text makes sense and flows well; none is missing and none is repeated.   ☐ ☐
- Wording is clear, in general *and for intended audience.   ☐ ☐
- Technical concepts are explained clearly.   ☐ ☐

Spelling and Capitalization
- Spelling and usage of common words are correct.   ☐ ☐
- Spelling and capitalization of proper names and special terms are consistent.   ☐ ☐
- Abbreviations and acronyms are spelled consistently and defined as appropriate.   ☐ ☐
- Product names, trademarks, and registered trademarks are verified.   ☐ ☐
- Capitalization following colons is accurate and consistent.   ☐ ☐

Grammar
- Subjects and verbs agree.   ☐ ☐
- Verbs are in correct tense.   ☐ ☐
- Pronouns agree with their antecedents and are in correct case.   ☐ ☐
- Modifiers are placed to keep meanings clear.   ☐ ☐

Punctuation
- There is no missing, duplicated, or misplaced punctuation.   ☐ ☐
- Apostrophes are used only for possessives and missing letters and face the correct way.   ☐ ☐
- If used, series commas appear consistently.   ☐
- A comma, without a connecting conjunction, is not used to separate two complete sentences (use stronger punctuation instead).   ☐ ☐
- Em and en dashes are used correctly and spaced consistently.   ☐ ☐
- Hyphenations and word divisions are correct and consistent.   ☐ ☐
- There are opening *and* closing parentheses, brackets, and quotation marks.   ☐ ☐
- Period is inside parentheses when ending a separate and complete sentence; outside when the parenthetical matter—even a complete sentence—is included in another sentence.   ☐ ☐
- Double and single quotation marks are used correctly.   ☐ ☐
- Periods and commas are inside quotation marks; semicolons and colons are outside; other punctuation is inside or outside as appropriate to context.   ☐ ☐

Numbers
- Numbers are treated consistently (either spelled out or numerals).   ☐ ☐
- Styles for area codes, phone numbers, dates, times, etc., are consistent.   ☐ ☐

Spacing
- There is one (and only one) space between words and following periods and colons.   ☐ ☐

Fonts and Symbols
- Italic and other special fonts are used consistently.   ☐ ☐
- Icons and symbols are used consistently.   ☐ ☐

References and Links
- Text references to figures, tables, and other elements are present and accurate.   ☐ ☐
- Directional references ("above" and "below") and cross-references to other parts of the document are correct.   ☐ ☐
- In electronic copy, Web and internal links work correctly.   ☐ ☐

continued

Professional 8-Stage Proofreading Checklist *(continued)*	✔ First Reading	✔ Second Reading

Stage 2: Section Numbers and Titles
- Typeface, spacing, and placement are consistent. ☐ ☐
- Any numbering is consecutive and in appropriate form (e.g., all roman or all arabic). ☐ ☐
- Spelling, capitalization, and hyphenation are correct and consistent. ☐ ☐
  - First letter after colons is capitalized; first letter after em dashes is capitalized or not per style guidelines. ☐ ☐
  - Articles, conjunctions, and prepositions are lowercased, unless starting or ending a title or contrary to desired style. ☐ ☐
  - First word and last word are capitalized, regardless of part of speech. ☐ ☐
  - First word following a hyphen is initial-capped or lowercase per style guidelines. ☐ ☐

Stage 3: Text Headings
- *Heading levels reflect correct hierarchy. ☐ ☐
- *Headings accurately reflect the content they introduce. ☐ ☐
- *Heading style is consistent for each level (e.g., all third-level headings use active voice). ☐ ☐
- Typeface, spacing, and placement are consistent for each heading level. ☐ ☐
- Spelling, capitalization, and hyphenation are correct and consistent. ☐ ☐
  - First letter after colons is capitalized; first letter after em dashes is capitalized or not per style guidelines. ☐ ☐
  - Articles, conjunctions, and prepositions are lowercased, unless starting or ending a heading or contrary to desired style. ☐ ☐
  - First word and last word are capitalized, regardless of part of speech. ☐ ☐
  - First word following a hyphen is initial-capped or lowercase per style guidelines. ☐ ☐

Stage 4: Lists and Tables
- Punctuation at end of text introducing lists and tables is consistent per style guidelines. ☐ ☐
- *Bulleted lists are used when sequence is unimportant or for sublists in numbered lists. ☐ ☐
- *Unless content dictates another order, bulleted list items are alphabetical. ☐ ☐
- *Numbered lists are used to indicate sequence. ☐ ☐
- Numbering in each list is sequential and starts at 1 or A. ☐ ☐
- Typeface, spacing, and placement of table headings and text are consistent. ☐ ☐
- Bullet styles and numeral typefaces are consistent. ☐ ☐
- Placement (flush left, indented, etc.) of lists and tables is consistent. ☐ ☐
- Alignment of runover text and right margin style in list items are consistent. ☐ ☐
- Space between bullet or numeral and start of text is consistent. ☐ ☐
- Initial capitalization of list items is consistent per style guidelines. ☐ ☐
- Typeface and punctuation of list item lead-ins are consistent. ☐ ☐
- Punctuation at end of list items is consistent per style guidelines. ☐ ☐
- Spacing around lists and tables is consistent. ☐ ☐

Stage 5: Captions and Art Labels
- Typeface, spacing, and placement of captions and labels are consistent. ☐ ☐
- Numbered captions and labels are in consecutive order. ☐ ☐
- Spelling, capitalization, and punctuation are correct and consistent. ☐ ☐
- Captions and labels accurately describe graphics. ☐ ☐

Professional 8-Stage Proofreading Checklist *(continued)*	✔ First Reading	✔ Second Reading
Stage 6: Page Numbers, Headers, and Footers		
• Typeface, spacing, and placement are consistent.	☐	☐
• Left and right (verso and recto) design and content are applied consistently.	☐	☐
• Spelling, capitalization, and hyphenation are correct and consistent.	☐	☐
• Content of headers/footers is correct for each section.	☐	☐
• Page numbering is consecutive overall or within sections, as appropriate, and appears on all pages where it should.	☐	☐
Stage 7: Table of Contents		
• Listings exactly match text headings.	☐	☐
• No headings of appropriate level are omitted; no inappropriate ones are included.	☐	☐
• Formatting (typeface, spacing, leaders, indents, etc.) of listings is consistent for each level shown.	☐	☐
• In print documents, all page numbers are present and correct.	☐	☐
• In electronic or Web documents, all links to named sections work correctly.	☐	☐
Stage 8: Final Look		
• There are no lines too short or too long.	☐	☐
• There are no stacked hyphens.	☐	☐
• White space and overall spacing are appropriate.	☐	☐
• *Overall layout is pleasing and presents content effectively.	☐	☐
• A final spell-check produces no errors.	☐	☐
• A search for double spaces shows no extra spaces.	☐	☐
• In Web documents, navigation buttons work correctly.	☐	☐

Complete Editorial Checklist

The checklist that follows brings together the three individual checklists that appear at the end of Chapters 3, 4, and 5, to provide you with reminders—in a single place—that cover all aspects of editing. Keep it handy and refer to it often to ensure that the writing you edit is the best it can be.

Complete Editorial Checklist	✔ First Reading	✔ Second Reading

Is It Correct?

Spelling and Capitalization

• Proper nouns, common words, and special terms are spelled and capitalized correctly.	☐	☐
• Shortened forms (abbreviations and acronyms) are spelled and capitalized correctly and defined when first used or as needed.	☐	☐
• Product names, trademarks, and registered trademarks are verified.	☐	☐
• Titles, including the first and last word, are capitalized correctly.	☐	☐
• Capitalization following colons in text is accurate:		
-Unless a proper name, lowercase when colon introduces less than a full sentence	☐	☐
-Consistently lowercase (unless a proper name) *or* capital letter when colon introduces a single sentence	☐	☐
-Capital letter when colon introduces two or more sentences	☐	☐

Grammar

• Subjects and verbs agree (*I work, he works*).	☐	☐
• Verbs are in correct tense (*I work, I worked, I had worked*, etc.).	☐	☐
• Pronouns agree in gender and number with what (or whom) they refer to (*Tom and Bill rode **their** bikes; the tree dropped **its** leaves*).	☐	☐
• Pronouns are correct according to their place in the sentence (***I** gave it to **him**; he gave it to **me***).	☐	☐
• Adjectives and adverbs are placed to keep meanings clear (*I drive on Friday **only*** [other days, I walk]; *I **only** drive on Friday* [and do nothing else all day]).	☐	☐

Punctuation

General

• There is no missing punctuation.	☐	☐
• There is no duplicated or misplaced punctuation.	☐	☐

Apostrophes

• Apostrophes are used only for possessives (*Jane's*) and missing letters (*I'll; rock 'n' roll*), not for plurals (*two Janes; 1900s*).	☐	☐
• Apostrophes face the correct way (*'04*, not *'04*).	☐	☐

Commas

• A comma is used before the last item in a series (*Tom, Dick, and Harry*), unless chosen style omits it.	☐	☐
• A comma, without a connecting conjunction, is not used to separate two complete sentences (use stronger punctuation, like a period or semicolon, instead).	☐	☐

Dashes

• Em dashes (—) are used correctly—in pairs if they're in the middle of a sentence (consistently with spaces or not)—to set off words and are the width of a capital *M*.	☐	☐
• To replace the word *to* or *through*, an en dash (–) is used (with no spaces) to separate items in ranges (*London–Paris, 7 a.m.–9 a.m., 1999–2004*) and is half the width of an em dash.	☐	☐

Hyphens

• Hyphenations and word divisions are correct (check a dictionary).	☐	☐

Complete Editorial Checklist *(continued)*	✔ First Reading	✔ Second Reading
Parentheses and Brackets		
• There are always opening *and* closing parentheses and brackets.	☐	☐
Periods		
• Period is *inside* parentheses when they enclose a separate and complete sentence.	☐	☐
• Period is *outside* parentheses when the parenthetical matter—even a complete sentence—is included in *another* sentence.	☐	☐
Quotation Marks		
• There are always opening *and* closing quotation marks as appropriate.	☐	☐
• Single quotation marks are used only around a quote within a quote.	☐	☐
• Periods and commas are inside quotation marks.	☐	☐
• Semicolons and colons are outside quotation marks.	☐	☐
• Other punctuation is inside or outside quotation marks, depending on whether it's part of the quoted item.	☐	☐
Lists		
• Numbered lists are used when sequence matters or items will be cited.	☐	☐
• Bulleted lists are used when sequence is unimportant and citation is unnecessary.	☐	☐
Figures, Graphs, and Art		
• Text references to figures, tables, and other elements are accurate and present as needed.	☐	☐
• Captions accurately describe graphics.	☐	☐
Sequence		
• Numbering in each numbered list is sequential and starts at 1 or A.	☐	☐
• Bulleted list items are in alphabetical order (unless another order makes more sense).	☐	☐
• Any section title numbering is consecutive.	☐	☐
• Heading levels (first, second, third, etc.) are styled correctly for the content they introduce.	☐	☐
• Numbered captions are in consecutive order.	☐	☐
• Page numbering is consecutive overall or within sections, as appropriate, and appears on all pages where it should.	☐	☐
Spacing		
• Words are separated by one (and only one) space.	☐	☐
• Periods and colons are followed by only one space.	☐	☐
Titles, Headers, and Footers		
• Titles and other headings accurately describe the content they introduce.	☐	☐
• Content of headers (at the top of the page) and footers (at the bottom) is correct for each section.	☐	☐
• Any numbering is consecutive and in appropriate form (e.g., all roman or all arabic).	☐	☐
• Spelling and capitalization are correct and consistent:		
-First letter after a colon is capitalized.	☐	☐
-First letter after an em dash or hyphen is capitalized or not, per style guidelines.	☐	☐

continued

Complete Editorial Checklist *(continued)*	✔ First Reading	✔ Second Reading
-Articles, short conjunctions, and short prepositions are lowercased, unless starting or ending a title, or contrary to style guidelines.	☐	☐
-First and last word are capitalized, regardless of part of speech.	☐	☐

Table of Contents

• Entries exactly match headings that appear in the document.	☐	☐
• All headings appear that should (all first-level, all second-level, etc.); none appear that shouldn't.	☐	☐
• In electronic and Web documents, all links between table of contents and text sections work correctly.	☐	☐

Web Links

• In electronic copy, Web links in text work correctly.	☐	☐

Is It Consistent?

Watch for consistency in . . .

• Statements of fact	☐	☐
• Spelling (especially in acronyms and other all-capital items)	☐	☐
• Capitalization (especially in titles, abbreviations, acronyms, and following colons)	☐	☐
• Hyphenations and word divisions	☐	☐
• Last comma (or no last comma) in a series of items; commas or no commas around *Jr., Sr., Inc.,* etc.	☐	☐
• Numbers—either spelled out or numerals, and consistent style for area codes, phone numbers, dates, times, etc.	☐	☐
• Italic and other special fonts	☐	☐
• Icons and symbols	☐	☐
• Lists and tables:		
-Punctuation at the end of text that introduces the list or table	☐	☐
-Bullet and number styles	☐	☐
-Indents, spacing, and alignment	☐	☐
-Capital letters (or lowercase) at the start of each item	☐	☐
-Font, capitalization, and punctuation of list item lead-ins	☐	☐
-Punctuation at end of list items (either periods or no periods)	☐	☐
-Parallel structure	☐	☐
-Table title numbering (or not) and style	☐	☐
-Table-specific abbreviations (including numbers)	☐	☐
-Headings (and *continued* lines) for multipage tables	☐	☐
-Table placement and format styles	☐	☐
• Document titles and headings	☐	☐
• Captions and labels	☐	☐
• Page numbers, headers, and footers	☐	☐
• Table of contents entries	☐	☐

Is It Clear and Compelling?

Sense, Flow, and Effectiveness

• The level of writing is appropriate for the audience.	☐	☐
• The piece has an effective beginning, middle, and end.	☐	☐
• The sequence of topics is logical and effective.	☐	☐

Complete Editorial Checklist *(continued)*	✔ First Reading	✔ Second Reading
• The language is not overly complex or wordy.	☐	☐
• The tone is respectful and free of bias.	☐	☐
• Wording is clear, and technical concepts and special terms are explained as appropriate.	☐	☐
• Conclusions flow logically from stated facts.	☐	☐
• Common words and expressions are used idiomatically.	☐	☐
• Pronouns have clear antecedents.	☐	☐
• Lists have parallel structure.	☐	☐
• Transitions are clear, graceful, and well placed.	☐	☐
• The writing contains strong images and active constructions.	☐	☐
• There is no ambiguity.	☐	☐
• There is no redundancy or repetition.	☐	☐
• Sentences vary in length and structure.	☐	☐
• There are neither too many nor too few paragraph breaks.	☐	☐
• Vertical lists or tables, rather than paragraphs, itemize information where appropriate.	☐	☐
• Examples and illustrations appear where needed.	☐	☐
• Any humor is appropriate and tasteful.	☐	☐

Glossary

abbreviations, acronyms, and initialisms. An abbreviation is a shortened form of a word, an acronym is a term that's made from the first letters of a phrase and pronounced as a single word, and an initialism is an acronym that's pronounced letter by letter.

ascender. The part of a lowercase letter that extends above the body of the letter.

balloon. *In Microsoft Word*, the name for an oblong box in the margin of a page in which your changes can be presented and comments can be inserted.

banner. *On the Web*, a typically rectangular advertisement on a Web page. It is often linked to an advertiser's own Web site.

browser. A software application used to locate and display Web pages.

buckslip. *In advertising*, one or more small inserts—about the size of a dollar bill—included with a letter or brochure.

captions and labels. Captions appear *near* illustrations, usually below them. Labels appear *within* illustrations to point out specific features.

caret. The editorial symbol used to indicate where an insertion is to be made in a line of text.

code. The written instructions that make computer software do what it does.

default. *In software applications,* a value or setting that a program automatically selects if you do not specify a substitute.

descender. The part of a lowercase letter that extends below the body of the letter.

dialog box. A box that appears on a computer screen to present information or request input. Typically, it is temporary, and disappears once you have entered the requested information and clicked OK (or some equivalent).

download. To copy a file from a main source (often via a link on a Web site) to your computer. The opposite is **upload**, which means to copy a file from your own computer to another location.

dynamic. *On the Web,* text or graphics that move, for example, animations. Dynamic text moves, but the user has no control over it and does not affect it in any way.

editing, levels of. Editorial tasks fall on a continuum, with proofreading at one end and substantive editing at the other:

> **standard proofreading.** Makes sure writing is free of mechanical errors—in spelling, punctuation, consistency, and some elements of formatting—and is grammatically correct.

> **editorial proofreading.** Encompasses all the tasks in standard proofreading and also includes a few minor tweaks to ensure clarity and correct word choice.

> **copyediting.** Involves all proofreading tasks and also improves phrasing and organization to make the writing more effective.

> **substantive editing.** Calls for a greater level of rewriting and reorganization and even for suggesting new approaches and ideas.

editors'/proofreaders' marks. Widely known and understood symbols used to mark errors and changes on hard-copy documents.

electronic format. Material in a form that can be sent or received electronically; for example, via e-mail.

em dash (—). A dash the width of a capital *M* in whatever typeface you're using. It signals breaking news—a whole new thought, more information, or an explanation.

en dash (–). A dash half the width of an em dash. It's most often used in a range of dates, times, and numbers.

external hard drive. A hard drive (available in various sizes) that is separate from your computer. A great option to use to back up items from your main computer.

field. *In software applications or on Web pages,* a space allocated for a particular item of information; for example, a name field on an order form.

flush-and-hang. See **hanging indent, hanging indentation.**

folio. Page number.

font. A complete assortment of a given size and style of type, including caps, small caps, lowercase, punctuation marks, accents, and commonly used symbols.

FTP (File Transfer Protocol). A protocol for exchanging files over the Internet instead of by e-mail—especially useful when transferring extremely large files.

function. *In software applications,* an item that appears in the menu. Also sometimes called an **option** or mode.

GUI (graphical user interface). A program interface that takes advantage of the computer's graphics capabilities to make the program easier to use. Basic GUI components: pointer, pointing device, icons, desktop, windows, and menus.

gutter. The two abutted inner margins of facing pages of a book.

hanging indent, hanging indentation. Type set with the first line of the paragraph flush left, and the lines following it indented. Also known as **flush-and-hang** style.

hard copy. Anything printed on paper.

headers and footers. Text at the top or bottom, respectively, of pages, such as the title of the document, page numbers, and so on.

HTML (HyperText Markup Language). An authoring language used to create documents on the Web. HTML defines the structure and layout of a Web document by using a variety of tags and attributes.

interactive features. *In software applications,* features that the user has some control over or can manipulate to get a response.

justification. The adjustment of the spacing within lines of type to fit the lines to a specific measure on the type page. Justified type has even margins on both sides. Compare **ragged right.**

key equivalent. *In software applications,* a combination of keys used to perform a function that can also be performed by clicking an onscreen option.

mirror margins. Margins used for documents that will be bound book style. The margins on the inside of a **spread** are slightly wider than the outside margins, to allow all margins to appear the same once the pages are bound.

option. *In software applications,* an addition to a command that changes or refines the command in a specified manner.

orphan. A short line appearing at the bottom of a page, or a word or part of a word appearing on a line by itself at the end of a paragraph. Compare **widow.**

path. *In software applications,* the route to a particular function; for example, File > Save.

PDF (Portable Document Format). The format in which a file in Adobe Acrobat is saved. A PDF file will appear exactly as its creator intended it to, regardless of who reads it or what platform displays it. And in most cases no one else can directly alter that file.

point. The basic unit of typographical measurement, equal to $1/72$ of an inch.

portrait or landscape. In printing on a letter- or legal-size sheet of paper, *portrait* means the sheet is positioned vertically (with the shorter edge at the top), and *landscape* means printing with the sheet placed horizontally (with the longer edge at the top).

POS (Point of Sale). The physical location at which goods are sold to customers.

product identifiers, product numbers. *In catalogs*, letters or numbers designating a pictured item and the corresponding description.

query. A question from an editor to an author.

ragged right. Type that has equal spaces between all words and so breaks at slightly different locations along the right-hand margin. Compare **justification**.

resolution, screen resolution. The number of pixels displayed on a computer screen; affects the sharpness of displayed images.

river. *In editing*, an undesirable streak of white space running more or less vertically through several lines of type.

roman. The "standard" text style—with no italics, boldface, or other special treatment.

run in. To merge a paragraph or line with the preceding one.

running feet. Copy set at the bottom of printed pages.

running heads. Copy set at the top of printed pages.

runover, turnover. Lines other than the first line in a **flush-and-hang** paragraph.

screen capture. A copy of what is currently displayed on a computer screen.

scroll bar. *In software applications or on the Web*, a narrow bar that appears on the side or bottom of a window that lets the user control which part of a document is currently visible.

SKU (Stock Keeping Unit). A common term for a unique numeric identifier used to refer to a specific product in inventory or in a catalog.

small caps. An abbreviation for small capitals—capital letters equal to the height of the lowercase letters without **ascenders** or **descenders**.

smart quotes. Microsoft's term for apostrophes and quotation marks that are curly as opposed to straight.

spread. Two facing pages.

static text. *In software applications and on the Web*, text that doesn't move—like the words on this page.

stet. A term most often used when marking hard copy, meaning to ignore a noted change and return the text to its original form.

style. *In software applications*, the fonts and formatting applied to elements in text. For example, a Heading 1 in Word might be Times New Roman, boldface, 24 pt.

style sheet. A listing of things an editor needs to remember and keep consistent while working on a piece of writing. Style sheets can be made for documents, clients or departments, or whole organizations (a house style sheet). In case they conflict, client or department style sheets trump house style sheets, and document style sheets trump both.

toolbar. *In software applications*, an onscreen strip that contains clickable items (buttons or menu options) that perform specific functions.

Track Changes. The feature in Word that allows you to show all your suggested changes and queries in a way that's easily distinguished from the rest of the text. Anyone reviewing your work can then accept or reject the changes.

TSP (Typeface, Spacing, Placement). A trio of items to be aware of as you maintain consistency in titles and headings, lists, tables, captions, labels, page numbers, headers, footers, and tables of contents.

typeface. A collection of fonts with common design or style characteristics; for example, Times New Roman. May include roman, italic, boldface, condensed, and other fonts.

upload. To copy a file from your computer to another location via the Internet.

URL (Uniform Resource Locator). The address of a Web location.

Webdings, Wingdings. Two fonts that contain symbols and pictures instead of numbers, letters, and punctuation.

widow. A short line of text appearing alone at the top of a page. Compare **orphan.**

For Reference and Reading

As we edit, we keep learning; you will, too. Experience is a great teacher, and so is the collection of books that follows. This list contains a few of the many sources you can turn to as you further your own education.

The American Heritage Dictionary of the English Language, 4th ed. Houghton Mifflin, 2000.

The Art of Styling Sentences, 4th ed. Ann Longknife and K.D. Sullivan. Barron's, 2002.

The Associated Press Stylebook. Associated Press. Basic Books, 2004.

The Careful Writer. Theodore M. Bernstein. Atheneum, 1995.

The Chicago Manual of Style: The Essential Guide for Writers, Editors, and Publishers, 15th ed. University of Chicago Press, 2003.

The Copyeditor's Handbook: A Guide for Book Publishing and Corporate Communications, 2nd ed. Amy Einsohn. University of California Press, 2005.

Edit Yourself: A Manual for Everyone Who Works with Words. Bruce Ross-Larson. W. W. Norton & Company, 1982.

The Elements of Style, 4th ed. William Strunk and E. B. White. Longman, 1999.

The Elephants of Style: A Trunkload of Tips on the Big Issues and Gray Areas of Contemporary American English. Bill Walsh. McGraw-Hill, 2004.

The Fine Art of Copyediting, 2nd ed. Elsie Myers Stainton. Columbia University Press, 2002.

Garner's Modern American Usage. Bryan A. Garner. Oxford University Press, 2003.

Go Ahead . . . Proof It! K.D. Sullivan. Barron's, 1996.

The Gremlins of Grammar. Toni Boyle and K.D. Sullivan. McGraw-Hill, 2005.

Lapsing Into a Comma. Bill Walsh. Contemporary Books, 2000.

Merriam-Webster's Collegiate Dictionary, 11th ed. Merriam-Webster, Inc., 2003.

Modern American Usage: A Guide. Wilson Follet. Hill & Wang, 1998.

Woe Is I: The Grammarphobe's Guide to Better English in Plain English. Patricia T. O'Conner. Riverhead Books, 2003.

Word Court. Barbara Wallraff. Harcourt, Inc., 2000.

Words Fail Me: What Everyone Who Writes Should Know About Writing. Patricia T. O'Conner. Harvest-HBJ Books, 2000.

Words Into Type, 3rd ed. Marjorie E. Skillin and Robert M. Gay. Prentice-Hall, 1974.

Your Own Words. Barbara Wallraff. Counterpoint Press, 2004.

Index